The
Positive
Power
of
Negative
Emotions

How harnessing your darker feelings can help you see a brighter dawn

TIM LOMAS

piatkus

PIATKUS

First published in Great Britain in 2016 by Piatkus

1 3 5 7 9 10 8 6 4 2

A CIP catalogue record for this book
is available from the British Library.

Note: the names of people featured in the case studies
have been changed to protect their privacy.

ISBN 978-0-349-41284-9

Typeset in Stone Serif by M Rules
Printed and bound in Great Britain by
Clays Ltd, St Ives plc

Papers used by Piatkus are from well-managed forests
and other responsible sources.

MIX
Paper from
responsible sources
FSC® C104740

Piatkus
An imprint of
Little, Brown Book Group
Carmelite House
50 Victoria Embankment
London EC4Y 0DZ

An Hachette UK Company
www.hachette.co.uk

www.improvementzone.co.uk

Dedication

To Kate and the whole family

Contents

Acknowledgements

I would like to thank some people who are very important to me, and without whom this book would not have been possible. First of all, my amazing wife, love of my life, and the sunshine who lights up my world – thank you just for everything! All my love and thanks to my dear mum, dad, brother and sister, who are the best, most loving family a person could wish for. Much love to my wonderful extended family in Liverpool and the United States as well. I'd also like to thank my students and colleagues at the University of East London, particularly Kate Hefferon and Itai Ivtzan, for their encouragement and support over recent years. Wholehearted thanks to my fantastic agent, Esmond Harmsworth, without whose guidance this book would never have happened. Likewise, my immense gratitude to my incredible editor, Claudia Connal, and to all the team at Piatkus; I'm truly thankful to you for taking a chance on me, and helping me make the book as good as possible. Finally, thanks to all my great friends for their companionship and care throughout the years. I owe a huge debt of gratitude to everyone mentioned here, and could not have written this book without you. This is dedicated to you all, with love.

Introduction

We all want to feel happy. We all yearn to be free of pain and suffering, to have blessed moments of love and laughter, to make the most of our brief sojourn on Earth. These longings are constants at the heart of human existence. We're therefore tantalised by an ever-expanding array of possible pathways towards these evanescent goals, shimmering ahead of us like oases in a scorching desert. Bookshops are heaving with self-help literature promising us the secret of happiness. Social media is likewise abuzz with the seductive voices of gurus who confidently promise to lead us there. Indeed, my own field of positive psychology – the scientific study of wellbeing – has provided much of the theory and research behind all this. Alluringly, we're promised that if we can just capture that optimistic mindset, or forge that precious set of meaningful relationships, then the end of the rainbow is just around the corner. And when we reach it, the rewards are apparently bountiful. Happiness is depicted as a golden key that can unlock innumerable delectable treasures – from success to good health.

This is a beautiful vision. And research does indeed suggest that happiness is connected to psychological qualities

like optimism, and to life circumstances such as close relationships. Then, if people *are* happy, there is evidence that it
can lead to other rewards – from ascending more swiftly up
a career ladder to finding that soulmate who gives reason to
our days.

The trouble is, however, that the blessings of happiness
can be elusive, and the 'positive' qualities that take us there
can be fiendishly difficult to capture. Many of us can't just
tune into the requisite brightness of spirit or upbeat state of
mind, which is why we are turning to the self-help shelves
in our droves, lost and confused. We have our moments in
the sun, of course – fleeting blessings of joy and laughter. All
too frequently, though, we struggle through the mist, beset
by worries, fears and lamentations. It's all very well knowing
that optimism is the route to happiness, and happiness the
doorway to health and success. But if we are unable to shake
that anxious pessimism, then where does that leave us? We
may feel even worse than before: experiencing anxiety is bad
enough, but being told we should be bright and upbeat just
deepens our worries. We start to feel anxious about feeling
anxious, or feel sad about feeling sad, so down and down we
go, in a dispiriting spiral . . .

Redeeming the Darkness

If any of the above rings true, if you are wearily familiar with
the darker shades of human experience, then this book has a
revolutionary and uplifting message for you. Your 'negative'
feelings are not only normal and natural but may serve as
pathways to the very happiness and flourishing that you seek.

Such emotions are not 'wrong', and we are not disordered or ill if we experience them. It is entirely natural to feel sad, angry, anxious and so on. Indeed, these emotions are not only normal but often entirely *appropriate*. It is surely right to feel sad if we lose somebody, or angry if we've been hurt. These are 'right' emotions in the sense that it would be rather inappropriate to feel unreservedly happy if we've suffered bereavement or betrayal. Moreover, not only are these darker emotions frequently natural and appropriate; they may be wellsprings of real value. As painful as they can feel at the time, they might conceal powerful messages and energies that can help us towards the light – towards the dawn of happiness. So, if we learn from them, and use them skilfully, our darker emotions may be strange and unexpected sources of salvation.

I should emphasise that I am not talking here about mental illnesses, like depression. It would be an affront for me to romanticise the plight of people who suffer with such debilitating conditions, or to claim that their burden is not serious. That said, I would not be so presumptuous as to suggest that their suffering *lacks* value, or to assert that illness cannot confer certain qualities upon the sufferer that they may come to appreciate, such as empathic sensitivity towards others. People may find redemption and meaning in all kinds of ways, even in the midst of great distress and illness. Either way, though, this is not a book about mental illness, but simply about the 'normal' darker emotions that we all feel from time to time – from sadness to anger.

Of course, how we differentiate mental illness from 'normal' emotions – where we draw the line – is itself a complex and contentious issue. Nevertheless, as I proceed through this book, I shall offer suggestions as to where this line might be, and what to do if you feel you have crossed it. In general, I follow the line drawn by the American Psychiatric Association – namely, their criteria for what constitutes a mental disorder. The criteria for depression and anxiety – the two most common mental illnesses – are outlined at the end of the book, in the Further Help and Resources section. For other mental illnesses, the criteria can be found in the websites provided in this section. Readers who are concerned that they may have crossed the line – with respect to any illness – are encouraged to check with their doctor, who will be able to offer appropriate guidance and support.

This book, then, deals with the vague, troubling territory that is captured by the phrase 'negative emotions'. These are the darker feelings that can descend on us all – from sadness and anxiety to guilt and loneliness. Unless a certain line of severity is crossed, these are *not* mental illnesses, but rather inherent dimensions of the human condition. More than that, however, as I intimated above, they are not merely normal, natural and appropriate. In a subtle, somewhat paradoxical way, they might be pathways to deeper and richer forms of wellbeing than may be found through more overtly 'positive' emotions. For example, sadness may open our hearts to the fragile beauty of life, or make us reach out to others in love and compassion, while righteous anger can alert us to some moral breach and motivate us to fight against an unjust social situation, changing it for the better.

We may not *choose* to experience these negative emotions. But if we do, and if we harness them skilfully, we might find that they can help us flourish, just as darkness gives way to the promise of the dawn.

The Path

As such, this book will take you on a revelatory and ultimately uplifting journey through some of the darker realms of the human experience. Although the road may be hard in places, we shall see that the shadows we so often walk through can contain surprising sources of solace and light. The book comprises eight chapters, each of which focuses on a specific negative emotion – namely, sadness, anxiety, anger, guilt, envy, boredom, loneliness and suffering. Each chapter centres on one overarching message, capturing the essence of that particular emotion, its main source of value. So, we shall see that sadness is fundamentally an expression of love and care. Anxiety is our alarm system, alerting us to danger. Anger can be a moral emotion that tells us that we've been treated unfairly. Guilt suggests that we have let ourselves down, and drives us to be better. Envy motivates us to improve ourselves and our lives. Boredom can be a gateway to creativity and self-transcendence. Loneliness allows our authentic voice to be heard, and teaches self-sufficiency. And suffering breaks us but then remakes us in potentially more meaningful ways.

The chapters then unpack these overarching lessons, teasing apart their elements. We begin with sadness, delving into the various ways in which it is a manifestation of loving concern – from a guardian that rescues us from a hurtful situation, to a precious connection to those we have loved and lost. We then explore how anxiety forewarns us about danger on the horizon and keeps us focused on current challenges. We shall also see that, far from signifying caution or even cowardice, anxiety is a natural response to stepping out of a comfort zone, and in the process developing as a person. Turning to anger, we see that this can be a moral emotion, a sign that we have been mistreated. However, we need to harness it carefully; otherwise, it can degenerate into corrosive feelings, such as hate. Consequently, the chapter considers how to use anger skilfully, as if meticulously prosecuting a crime – from diligently gathering evidence that allows us to present the case eloquently, to using wisdom and compassion as we endeavour to secure justice. In the next chapter, we learn that guilt takes the moral concern of anger and directs it at ourselves. As such, we explore the reasons why we sometimes pick the wrong path and find ourselves behaving badly. But these paths are not all equally wrong. So, while we may never be entirely guilt free, we can at least strive to develop 'better' forms of guilt, guided by more refined motivations.

Next comes envy, which likewise can be a motivating force, impelling us to improve ourselves and our lives. Our central task here is to move away from 'vicious' envy – where we simply resent people who have what we want – and towards 'emulative' envy, which inspires us to attain these desiderata for ourselves. Moreover, as with guilt, some needs are more elevated than others. As such, we can use this understanding to rise upwards and aim for higher goals. Moving on to boredom, the chapter undertakes a surprising reappraisal of this seemingly listless state. If we engage with boredom in the right spirit, it can be a gateway to mystery and intrigue – from facilitating creative impulses, to generating existential insights. The penultimate chapter then aims to make peace with loneliness by transforming it into the more contented state of solitude. This is possible when we appreciate that being alone may empower us to develop positive character traits, such as moral courage, and can even lead to elevated spiritual peaks. Finally, we address suffering itself – trauma or adversity that stirs up a dark combination of any or all of the seven emotions described above. With this, we encounter the redemptive possibility that we are tested through our trials and eventually remade in ways that we may come to appreciate.

Before we set off on the journey, just a brief word about the nature of the book. To illustrate the notion that each emotion contributes to wellbeing in numerous ways, I metaphorically imagine our inner world as being peopled by a host of figures. Each symbolises a particular aspect of a given emotion, and together they comprise its overarching essence. For instance, in Chapter 1, I introduce seven symbolic figures, each of which reflects a particular way in which sadness is an expression of love and care – from the *Nurse of Protection*, who keeps us from the fray until our wounds have healed, to the *Keeper of the Flame*, who safeguards our connections with people who have departed from our lives. These symbols should not be taken literally, of course. They do not imply some confused maze of dissociated voices, the 'multiple personalities' that are often associated with some forms of mental illness. Rather, they are the multi-coloured threads of the countless experiences, sights and sounds that we encounter on our journey through life and which, woven together, create our character. Our spirit speaks in different tones at certain times – tones that speak boldly of love, whisper longingly of hope, cry mournfully of loss. I have personified these tones by giving each a poetic label. These labels help us bring the valuable qualities of each emotion to life, and allow us to appreciate the subtle nuances that comprise its overarching value.

Within the framework provided by these symbolic figures, our travels will be illuminated by the personal stories
of people who have sought and/or discovered some value in
their darker emotions. I shall also draw on my own experiences, as I have known these feelings too, so I want to offer
my own testimony in a spirit of solidarity and companionship. In addition, our path will be guided by consideration
of cutting-edge scientific literature, which helps affirm the
insights found in the narratives.

Together, I hope that these elements will combine to create
an illuminating path through the darkness, and reveal that
even the blackest of nights may usher in the hopeful light of
dawn.

CHAPTER ONE

Sadness

At first glance, sadness may seem a daunting place from which to start our travels. Peering into this lonely valley, already our legs may feel heavy, a chill wrapping itself around our bones. Indeed, as my mind turns towards writing this chapter, I catch my breath, somewhat uneasy. I, like many people, often feel the breath of sorrow on my shoulder, and I'm wary of treading further into the darkness. And yet, we can perhaps most clearly discern this book's key message by beginning our tale with sadness: all of the darker emotions, including sadness itself, are not only normal but can be unexpected fonts of meaning and value.

This may sound surprising. On the surface, sadness can appear to be wholly unredeemable – a bleak, unforgiving state. Surely it is the very antithesis of happiness, a sheer absence of joy and pleasure. Well, yes, in one sense, sadness is indeed a dark, foreboding place, one which few people, if any, would voluntarily choose to visit. Therefore, I have no intention of being the mercurial, shady figure at the cross-roads, trying to 'sell' you sadness. My aim is not to make it appear alluring or even necessary, as if we *ought* to be sad. This is not a book about 'shoulds'. Goodness knows, we carry enough burdens – including pressures around how we should feel and act – without adding to our weight of expectation.

But if sadness does descend upon us, as it will for everyone from time to time, what then? Is it wrong? Should we be ashamed, chastised, even medicalised? Or might we make peace with it by acknowledging that it is often entirely natural and appropriate? That, paradoxically, it can even help us flourish.

Disentangling Sadness and Depression

In speaking of the potential virtues of *sadness*, I must right away emphasise that I am not talking about *depression*, which is a serious, damaging, debilitating illness. Indeed, the World Health Organisation has made the troubling forecast that depression will be second on the list of global disability burdens by 2020.[1] Of course, in attempting to differentiate between sadness and depression, the water immediately becomes murky, as the two conditions overlap in complicated ways. One common image is that of a spectrum, in which sadness shades into depression by degrees. Crucially, though, this does not imply a precarious, slippery slope, in which sadness is in constant danger of sliding inexorably towards depression. Rather, this idea of a spectrum presents sadness as normal and natural, an inherent – if unfortunate – aspect of the human condition. Then – if it becomes sufficiently intense and/or prolonged – it may cross the line into depression.[2] That moment is reached when something 'goes wrong' with sadness.[3] As to where the line might be, I would recommend following the guidelines set out by the American Psychiatric Association, which you can find in the Further Help and Resources section at the end of this book. Above all, if you are worried that you might be depressed – or, indeed, if you think you are suffering from any mental health issue – my advice is to consult your doctor, who will be able to offer the appropriate guidance and help.

Prior to the point when a person crosses the line into depression, however, it is important to see 'normal' sadness not as an illness but as part of our common humanity. It is one of the 'proper sorrows of the soul', in the words of the fourteenth-century monk Thomas à Kempis.[4] This is an important point, since we are in danger of medicalising the negative emotions that are discussed in this book, treating them as illnesses that should be 'cured' with drugs. For instance, in their book *The Loss of Sadness*, Anthony Horwitz and Jerome Wakefield argue that the quiet dignity of sadness is gradually being eroded and forgotten, subsumed within the medical concept of depression. With this erosion, which is driven by the influence of fields like psychiatry, sadness is liable to be seen simply as a mild form of depression – less problematic, certainly, but still undesirable and 'wrong'. In recent years Horwitz and Wakefield have led something of a counter-movement in the face of this insidious erosion of sadness. Their campaign has attempted to rehabilitate 'normal' sadness, differentiate it from the clinical illness that is depression, and acknowledge its rightful place at the table of common human emotions.

When normalising sadness in this way, an obvious place to start is with its unfortunate ubiquity and universality. No one is invulnerable to the vicissitudes of fate, to the life-shaking experiences of loss and bereavement. In such cases, sadness is an entirely appropriate response. Gentle reminders of the universality of such tragedies may then help foster a degree of acceptance – both of the loss itself and of sadness as the 'correct' response. The Buddha adopted this stance over 2500 years ago, and a similar approach has given solace to hundreds of millions of people ever since, both Buddhist and non-Buddhist. A grieving mother, Kisa Gotami, suffered the ultimate pain of losing her child. In desperation, she asked the Buddha for medicine that might bring her child miraculously back to life. With compassionate wisdom, the Buddha said that he could help. He asked Kisa to bring him a handful of mustard seeds, but made the seemingly strange stipulation that the seeds must be procured from a home where no one had ever lost a loved one. Kisa went forlornly from door to door, hoping to come across a household that had never suffered such a loss. Of course, every family had its own tale of woe, which they shared with Kisa, forging a connection in their shared sense of loss. This did not lessen Kisa's grief, but it did usher her into communion with others who had been left similarly bereft, showing her that it was only human to grieve as she was. She eventually attained a measure of acceptance about her loss, and understood that death is woven inherently into the fabric of existence.

In cultivating acceptance in this way, Buddhism speaks of 'two arrows'. When we lose someone, we are pierced by intense grief. This, or any other type of hurt, is the first arrow, which is wounding enough in itself. But all too often we also recoil against that initial reaction and start to feel sad about feeling sad (or, in another context, start to feel angry about feeling angry, for example). This secondary response – known in psychology as a 'meta-emotion' (that is, an emotion *about* an emotion) – is the second arrow. It can be just as hurtful as the first, and sometimes even more damaging. It may well be impossible to remove the first arrow, to temper the sense of loss or hurt we feel in experiences such as bereavement. However, if we can manage to accept our feelings – perhaps by seeing them as burdens we must all carry at some point in life – we can at least make peace with them and so remove the pain of the second arrow.

We do not have to be Buddhist to appreciate this notion of the two arrows. Indeed, Buddhism's ethos of acceptance is emphasised in almost every religious tradition, and in spiritual and therapeutic discourse more broadly. For instance, countless people from all walks of life and many faiths have received comfort and guidance from Reinhold Niebuhr's famous 'Serenity Prayer', which beautifully articulates the concept of acceptance:

> *God, grant me the serenity to accept the things I cannot change,*
> *The courage to change the things I can,*
> *And the wisdom to know the difference.*

Even if we treat sadness as 'normal', however, while this may help us make our peace with it, we might still regard it as an invidious, unwanted emotion. The simple fact that something is natural or normal does not necessarily lend it any justification or nobility. After all, illness is 'natural', but most people would surely wish it could be eradicated from their lives. Crucially, though, we can go further and potentially discern some *value* in sadness. Doing so is important, as it means we may not only accept the presence of sadness in our lives but learn to *appreciate* it, at least to some extent. We can realise that, despite its melancholic appearance, it can play a useful role in helping us lead full and fulfilling lives. Essentially, we become sad mainly when the people, places and even objects that we care about are threatened, hurt or lost. Seen in this way, we realise that sadness is primarily an expression of *love and care*.

To illustrate this idea, and to tease apart its nuances, I invite you to imagine your inner landscape peopled by a host of graceful, angelic figures. As explained in the Introduction, I am not implying anything unusual when speaking of such figures, or likening them to phenomena that are commonly associated with 'madness', such as hearing voices or multiple personalities. The figures are metaphorical, a series of poetic personifications of the various ways in which sadness operates within us as an expression of care. We shall meet seven such figures in this chapter. The first is the *Medic of the Battlefield*.

The Medic of the Battlefield

Sometimes sadness can seep in unnoticed, slowly filtering unobtrusively into our consciousness. At other times, it can hit sharply like a hammer blow, striking in a sudden moment of grief.

Like many people, I've suffered what must be one of the more common hurts: being discarded by a partner.

Although, in hindsight, this sorry incident was certainly not the end of the world, it did feel like it at the time. In my teenage years, I was captivated by my first girlfriend. I was naive, letting down friends, family and ultimately myself, sacrificing everything else to this new and exciting feeling. A fall was due, and it came. Aged eighteen, I followed her to a distant city as she began university. Within a week, she left me to join her new crowd. I plummeted down, tumbling into sadness. All those who have been similarly cast aside will know the pain I felt. Nor was the hurt fleeting; it haunted me for months.

Gradually, though, I began to rebuild myself. This was a slow, upward struggle, involving much soul-searching, tentative experiments with affection, an escape to China – which I'll speak of in the next chapter – and a gradual accumulation of confidence and strength. Before this, however, there were long months of darkness. It was a terrible time. The sadness I felt at being cut adrift was compounded by other jarring hurts: betrayal, confusion (I was lost in a maze of 'whys'), wounded self-esteem and drawn-out loneliness. Strangely, I stayed in that distant university city for three months, despite making few friends, in a kind of penitent, self-imposed exile, determined to hold out until Christmas. I worked part-time in a shoe shop (which I hated) and also had a short spell as a failed hotel barman (walking out ignomiously after just a few shifts, having managed to break a huge glass table). Other than that, I rarely left my flat. In other words, in the midst of my sadness and pain, I retreated from the world. This is the first role of sadness that we shall discuss here: self-preservation.

At times, life can be a battle, so inevitably we get wounded, especially by relationships. To return to the overall theme of this chapter, we are wounded because we care for someone else, because we love them; and that caring, that love, is a precious thing. But we also need to care for *ourselves*, and sadness can help with that. When we are at our most vulnerable, it makes us disengage and retreat, prompting us to seek refuge, away from the fray. The image this brings to mind is of a battlefield medic, working in the midst of a war zone to save incapacitated soldiers from further harm. When we've been hurt and our sadness makes us withdraw from the world, it is like our inner medic rushing to our side, saying, 'We need to get you away from this chaos', and spiriting us away to a safe place where we can recover our strength.

In psychology, this protective function is sometimes viewed as a form of mental pain,[5] with parallels to physical pain. It is easy to recognise the value of physical pain – the body's signal that a particular stimulus is harmful and/or we have suffered an injury, so protective, remedial action is needed. The physical pain we feel on touching a flame is the purest, most direct lesson we could have about the dangers of fire. Likewise, the pain we suffer from a burned hand is the body's way of saying that our flesh has been damaged, and needs attention. Consequently, we learn to be careful. The piercing emotional pain of sadness can sometimes serve a similar purpose. It is a visceral sign that a certain situation is harmful, and that we should withdraw to a safe distance. It is our inner field medic, evacuating us from the battle for our own protection. Without this inducement to retreat, we might otherwise stay right in the middle of harm's way, vulnerable to further damage.

My sadness eventually prompted me to give up on my

ex-girlfriend and cease the futile attempt to win her back. There was, of course, the odd desperate moment when I lunged out, tried to make contact and implored her to give us another chance, as if deliriously straining to return to the battle. These moments were few, though, and increasingly far between. Essentially, my sadness allowed me to quit the fight and relinquish what I knew was a lost cause. This was very important. While painful at the time, in the long run it was just what I needed. I had to suffer a sense of hopelessness about the relationship in order to remove myself, and eventually set myself on a better path.

One we have retreated, however, we must recuperate and recover. This is when our next avatar of sadness appears – the *Nurse of Protection*.

The Nurse of Protection

The *Medic* may have escorted us from the battlefield, out of harm's way, but what then? While retreating from the world for a time is beneficial, allowing such disconnection to become permanent can be dangerous. After all, most relationships are not fights, life is not usually a war zone, and we have plenty more living to do once we are ready. This doesn't mean we should try to 'forget' our losses. In the case of bereavement, say, grief might always be with us, and indeed might be a vital thread that links us to our lost loved ones (see the *Keeper of the Flame*, page 26). But we still need to pick ourselves up, dust ourselves down and carry on with our own journey. We keep walking, because that is what people do. Moreover, we walk in hope, since we don't know what welcoming, sunlit valley may be just over the horizon. On the other hand, if disengagement becomes enduring, if sadness becomes prolonged, we run the risk of falling into clinical depression.

I am not claiming to judge precisely when this point is reached. According to the American Psychiatric Association (APA), two weeks of continuous low mood, combined with other symptoms (such as a lack of energy), are grounds for a diagnosis of depression. But such rigid accounting may not always be appropriate. For instance, during my few months of sadness in the aftermath of my break-up, I may well have been *technically* depressed, according to the APA's guidelines. On the other hand, on hearing my story, rather than reaching such a diagnosis, a sensitive doctor might have viewed my melancholy as simply the natural reaction of a young man who felt bereft and lost. Hence, the 'acceptable' duration for sadness probably varies for every person and indeed for every situation. As ever, though, I would encourage you to see your doctor if you are worried that your sadness is becoming excessively intense and/or prolonged.

Of course, the hope is that we are eventually nursed back to health and feel able to rejoin the whirl of life. This comprises the second function of sadness: to keep us safe and protected while we recover our strength. While the *Medic of the Battlefield* whisked us out of harm's way, evacuating us from a painful situation, sadness can then ensure that we remain in our sanctuary until we are strong enough to return to action. In this respect, it is like a *Nurse of Protection*, caring for wounded soldiers until they are healthy enough to stand on their own two feet. Neurobiologists recognise this process as a form of 'hibernation'.[6] Just as some animals retreat from the harsh bitterness of winter, bedding down in the warmth of a swaddling nest, sadness can serve as a dark but ultimately rejuvenating cocoon. We huddle within it when we are wounded, conserving our resources and replenishing our energy. Sadness is also the reassuring, soft voice of the nurse, soothing us to sleep, bidding us to lie safe and sound until the rays of sunshine arrive.

Thus, sadness protects and shields us when we are at our most vulnerable. One powerful way in which it does this is by eliciting care from the people who are close to us. Picture a child, even one who is a stranger to you, breaking down in tears, their sadness obvious. How would you respond? Most of us would immediately try to help: the child's distress evokes the humane desire to reach out, to console, to assist. It is with good reason, then, that sadness and associated acts, including crying, are considered potent forms of 'signalling' behaviour.[7] Signalling is our interior world made visible, broadcasting our emotional state to those around us, alerting them to our distress. It draws in our protectors, care-givers and loved ones – guardian angels who watch over us and may nurse us back to health.

But sadness in this rehabilitative phase of protection and recovery doesn't only serve to elicit help. By entering hibernation, we are also afforded an opportunity to take stock and re-evaluate the events and choices that brought us to this low ebb in the first place. In bringing a temporary respite from our usual frantic inclinations to act and appear busy, sadness creates the time and space for the essential process of questioning. Sometimes we just need to stop in our tracks and ask some vital questions. Where am I going? Is this the right path for me? Why have I been marching this way? Having stopped, exhausted and vulnerable, we may even spot some fresh paths in the undergrowth that we would have strode straight past during the normal headlong dash through life. We see things we have never noticed before, and are gifted insights into understandings that were previously obscure. It is in these moments of clarity that we are visited by a third incarnation of sadness – the *Witness of Truth*.

The Witness of Truth

Sometimes the tears of sadness can make the scales fall from our eyes. They are like a long, dark monsoon that cleanses the earth, wiping away the accumulation of grime and dirt. We may start to see more clearly, and reorient ourselves towards the good. My sadness over losing my girlfriend made me see, with mournful but ultimately healing clarity, how wayward the relationship had been. I awoke to the truth of the matter: I needed to stand on my own feet, become my own person. Such realisations compelled me, even in my unsteady, sad state, to bid goodbye to the *Nurse of Protection* and make a bold leap into the future by embarking on a trip to China. I saw the path I needed to take – a path that I had been too preoccupied to discern before my fall. In sadness, then, we may become a *Witness of Truth*. This can feel painful at the time, but it is ultimately in our best interests.

The idea that sadness can generate greater clarity and awareness has been corroborated in the research laboratory, especially in an ingenious study conducted by two psychologists, Joseph Forgas and Rebekah East.[8] First, they arranged for two dozen undergraduates (students are often roped into these experiments!) to enter a room on campus. On the table was an envelope containing a cinema ticket, which the students were invited to either take or leave. Then, on leaving the room, all of the participants were instructed to deny taking the ticket in subsequent videotaped interviews with the researchers, irrespective of whether they had chosen to leave it on the table or not. As a result, Forgas and East recorded testimonies from both truth-tellers (those who had left the ticket on the table) and liars (those who had taken it). It was at this point that the crucial part of the experiment began. Forgas and East assembled another group of students and asked them to differentiate between the truth-tellers and the liars. Crucially, though, before watching the testimonies, this second group underwent one of three 'mood inductions', during which they watched a happy, a sad or a neutral film. It transpired that the melancholic students who had watched the sad movie were far better than the others at detecting the deception. Sadness served as their window on the truth.

This kind of witnessing may arise in all kinds of crises, opening our eyes to the reality of a situation and steering us on a different course. For instance, I was struck recently by the story of a young man we'll call Spencer, who found himself living the teenage dream when his band was signed to a major label and catapulted to stardom. For a few wild years, his life was electric – touring the world, sharing stages with his idols. But then, with Spencer still only in his early twenties, the label dropped the band and effectively ended Spencer's music career. That was not the end of his story, though.

Sometimes it is good to persevere – we take a punch, hit the floor, get back up and keep fighting. But at other times we need to accept that the fight is not worth it, that the odds are too stacked against us, that we should just walk away. Spencer must have felt great sadness when his dreams were so ruthlessly shattered. And yet, this sadness must have allowed him to see the record industry in all its stark, hardheaded reality. You may have experienced similar epiphanies during your low points – for example, the sobering recognition that your employer has no particular loyalty towards you, or the mournful realisation that a friend was just a fairweather companion. Armed with this newfound knowledge, Spencer did a brave and unusual thing: he walked away. He re-evaluated whether the pursuit of fame was the best path for him, and, with sober clarity, realised that it wasn't. With humility, he decided he needed more education, so he asked his old school if it would let him return to finish his qualifications. It agreed, so for a year he sat bashfully among the much younger kids. In doing so, he discovered aspects of himself that he had never realised he possessed, and depths of intelligence that had previously remained hidden. He did well enough to gain a place at university, and thereafter trained as a teacher. Now he is flourishing and inspiring others, a living testament to the power of sadness to set one's life on a better course.

So, as a *Witness of Truth*, we may find the strength to keep watch over our lives, guard against pitfalls and act in our own best interests. But this isn't all about us. When witnessing truth, we become sensitive to the travails of others too, and start to watch over them. This leads us to one of sadness's most important roles: the *Angel of Sorrow.*

The Angel of Sorrow

Last year, in Paris, I found myself drawn to Père Lachaise, a cemetery of such breathtaking size and grandeur that walking through its imposing wrought-iron gates is like entering a city of the dead. Cemeteries hold a mysterious power for me. Perhaps this is because, in their otherworldly stillness, the nagging stresses of everyday existence fade into insignificance, relativised when seen from the perspective of mortality. Or, maybe it is because these spectral places seem to exist in a slightly different plane of reality, unmoored from human time, cut adrift in the austere space of eternity. As my footsteps echoed on the cobbled path, I was transfixed by a large stone motif above a crumbling, unkempt tomb: a weeping angel. In my melancholy frame of mind, I imagined this ethereal being watching over the world and mourning its suffering. Yet, sorrowful as the image was, I was captivated by its beauty, as if it held some divine significance. Above all, at that moment, I was struck by the deep and mysterious bond between sadness and one of the most important human qualities: compassion.

In our sadness, we may witness many different truths – from the harsh realities of our chosen profession (as with Spencer) to deceptions by our peers. Above all, though, the sensitivity and insight that are conferred by sadness can heighten our awareness of suffering. We suddenly see the secret mark of loneliness in the neighbour we pass every day on the street. We notice the twinge of worry in a colleague's eye. We no longer shield our eyes from the beggar who huddles quietly in a doorway, discarded by society. We see the mistreatment of service workers, struggling to make a living at the margins of the city. This is not pity. We are not looking down condescendingly on those who are less fortunate than ourselves. Rather, in sadness, our hearts swell with compassion and channel the ethereal *Angel of Sorrow*. We not only recognise our kinship with these people, our shared suffering, but are compelled to reach out, to connect, and to offer our love and care.

The connection between sadness and compassion was brought home to me when I spent a few long years working as a nursing assistant in a psychiatric hospital. The job could be a rollercoaster: occasional outbursts of anger and aggression from distressed patients; long stretches of inactivity and boredom; even some laughter and fun, enjoying the odd game of dominoes or football. Above all else, though, the hospital was suffused by the suffering that the patients had to endure: tormented by voices, persecuted by self-hatred, or simply lost and alone in the world. I would not dare compare my sorrows to theirs, but I did have my own trials of sadness in there, especially during suicide watch – the most important aspect of my job. In some cases, it was sufficient to check on a patient every fifteen minutes. For some poor souls, though, a member of staff had to remain within arm's length at all times, so desperate was their wish to end it all. Occasionally the patient and I would discuss their plight, but often we would simply sit in silence.

My heart would feel so heavy at such times, with the sadness of the moment penetrating deep into my bones. These interactions tended to awaken my own dark melancholia, reflecting back my fears and sorrow, but they also felt mysteriously significant, as if a veil had been drawn back and I had stepped over the threshold into a sacred realm. Ordinary human concerns – the trivial hassles that clutter up our days – were suspended. Instead, there was just a quiet awareness of the terrifying mystery of life, of its preciousness and fragility. My sadness opened into a deep sense of connection with a fellow human being, and a feeling of compassion for their distress. And it was not just me who felt that way. I was surrounded by so many good-hearted members of staff who were likewise strongly moved by the plight of the people in our care. Indeed, while my nursing career was relatively brief, many of my colleagues had devoted their whole adult lives to caring for others. As such, I continually found inspiration and guidance in their example.

As this seam of compassion developed within me, I hoped that the patients were able to find some comfort in my presence ... although I always doubted my nursing ability and questioned my usefulness. Either way, though, during my years in the hospital I experienced moments of clarity and significance that I shall never forget. They felt intensely meaningful, as if I were serving some deeper purpose, one that was far more beneficial to the world than my usual selfish strivings. I know that many of my colleagues shared this outlook. Some spoke openly about it, particularly a few who were religious, for whom the work was a way of serving their faith. But I could tell that the others felt it too, even though they rarely discussed it. In these moments of connection, we all transcended our narrow, insular concerns and became part of something far greater than ourselves. Indeed, according to some scholars, this is the very definition of a purposeful life.[9]

Sometimes, however – perhaps most of the time – sadness is evoked by a person who is no longer with us. This is still very much an expression of love, though, and indeed is one of the most important voices of sadness: the *Keeper of the Flame*.

The Keeper of the Flame

Of all the causes of and reasons for sorrow, perhaps the hardest to bear, and yet tragically also the most common, is the loss of a loved one. As I write these words, I am acutely aware of how inadequate language is to convey the pain that is felt in bereavement, let alone begin to alleviate it. The heart needs to grieve, and to heal, in its own way and in its own time. I am even more wary of suggesting that there are 'benefits' in this grieving process. Although this book contains the uplifting message that seemingly negative emotions can be of great value, the last thing I want to do is dress up grief as a 'positive'. It may be the case that tragic events and other traumas can change lives in ways that are not *entirely* negative, such as bringing estranged family members back together, or deepening someone's spirituality. (These possibilities will be explored in the final chapter, when we consider the idea of 'post-traumatic growth', an inelegant phrase that jars with me but is now widely used to describe this kind of redemptive process.[10]) Nevertheless, bereavement and loss *are* sheer tragedies, and should be respected as such.

One thing I would like to do, however, is to reframe how we think about grief and the sorrow we feel when we lose someone. I wrote above about the unfortunate modern tendency for doctors to categorise sadness as a 'disorder', especially when it is prolonged, and then medicalise it as mild depression. Admittedly, the 'depression' label may be warranted in some severe cases of grief, but usually the sorrow that is experienced after a bereavement is inherently normal and appropriate. Moreover, in terms of reframing grief, one could argue that it is not a loss of love per se, but rather an *expression of* love. It is the way in which we continue to maintain a connection with our departed loved ones. From this perspective, sadness and joy are both manifestations of love, and indeed two sides of the same coin: love in the presence of its 'target' manifests as joy, and in its absence manifests as sadness.

Here, I am reminded of Robert M. Pirsig, author of the unsurpassable *Zen and the Art of Motorcycle Maintenance*. This book hit me like a thunderbolt when I was seventeen, and I must have read it half a dozen times since. It's a strange tale, written by an author of true but difficult genius. Essentially, it is a philosophical enquiry into the notion of 'quality', interwoven with a lightly fictionalised narrative of a road trip across Middle America that Pirsig took with his young son Chris, who was aged twelve at the time. For all its esoteric, head-spinning ideas, which certainly blew my teenage mind, it's the personal details that really hit you. Throughout the trip, Pirsig wrestles with his own demons, the ghosts of insanity, while struggling to connect with Chris and fulfil the responsibilities of fatherhood. By the end, though, there is a sense of resolution, and the book concludes with the optimistic words: 'It's going to get better now'.[11]

Tragically, it doesn't. My second-edition copy, published ten years after the first, contains an awful afterword which reveals that Chris was murdered outside a Zen centre when he was twenty-two years old. This news took my breath away, and a sense of bewilderment is evident in the writing. But then, with a kind of awkward grace, Pirsig suggests that Chris lives on, in a sense. He writes that the son he mourns was not so much a living 'object' as a 'pattern'. Part of this was his physical being, of course, but it was also way bigger than that, encompassing both father and son, everyone they knew, and even places and possessions. Grief is so tormenting because the centre of this pattern is suddenly wrenched away, and the remaining world seems unbearably empty. Yet Pirsig describes how, over time, he found meaning in maintaining, honouring and loving the larger pattern, even though its physical centre had disappeared. We keep the flame of love alive through this sorrow, so the person lives on too, in a way, cherished in our hearts.

Such sadness may become so important or meaningful that it can shape and define our character. It is in this sense that we see the penultimate guise of sadness: the *Engraver of Souls*.

The Engraver of Souls

That immortal poet of the human condition, the Lebanese-American Kahlil Gibran, once wrote, 'The deeper that sorrow carves into your being, the more joy you can contain'.[12] Something about this line resonates powerfully with me, and indeed with most others who read it. There is a profound truth in the idea that our sadness shapes the contours of our soul and the mettle of our character in a fundamental way. Just as an engraver uses force to carve incisions into stone, thereby creating an object of beauty, so our suffering makes each of us the unique individual that we are. Yet, Gibran is not merely saying that we each have a cross to bear, and that this burden helps define us. More radically, he is suggesting that there is a deep connection between sorrow and joy. It is as if our sadness creates the space for happiness to flow through, in the same way that an empty stage allows actors to sparkle in their element. Or, to use the central metaphor of this book, it is only because of the backdrop of darkness that the stars are able to shine forth, and the brightness of dawn is so welcome.

Countless people have taken solace in the idea that the darkest hour comes just before dawn. It speaks to a sense of hope, the redemptive possibility that suffering, like everything else, will pass, leading to the dawn of a brighter morning. Gibran's message goes further, though: the light exists and shines forth *because* of the darkness. Only when we are touched by sadness can we truly realise the power and value of happiness. Going further still, Gibran articulates the uplifting idea that the deeper the sadness we have endured, the greater the joy we are able to feel. This is not a justification for suffering or sadness: most people would surely prefer to live a life of pleasant ease, free of emotional peril. Yet, aside from the fact that a totally carefree existence is well-nigh impossible, in such a life we would probably have less *appreciation* of our happiness. Think of it as the contrast between a member of the aristocracy and someone who is born into poverty and then rises to the upper echelons of society. The aristocrat will probably take their wealth for granted, whereas the former pauper will remain acutely aware of how privileged their life has become.

Perhaps no one has explored these notions with as much eloquence as Jalāl ad-Dīn Muhammad Rūmī. Better known simply as Rumi, this thirteenth-century Persian scholar, mystic and poet was the author of some of the most timeless poetry ever written. His name also rings throughout history as the founder of the Mevlevi Order, a branch of the esoteric Sufi tradition (commonly known as 'Whirling Dervishes', for their unique practice of attaining an ecstatic spiritual state through meditative spinning). Born in present-day Afghanistan in 1207, Rumi spent much of his life in the sultanate of Rum, a state in Anatolia. Aged just twenty-five, he inherited the headship of a madrasa (a religious school) from his father – a highly respected official position. But in 1244 his life was shaken to the core when he met Shams-e Tabriz, an itinerant mystic. The two men immediately fell into a deep spiritual love and spent the next four years together in a state of intense happiness.

Then, in 1248, Shams suddenly disappeared, possibly murdered by some of Rumi's followers, who were likely jealous of the attention their master bestowed on him. In the decades that followed, Rumi created some of the most powerful love poetry ever written, at once ecstatic and heartbreaking. His deep longing for Shams was transformed into a spiritual quest, a transcendent hunger for union with the sacred. His poetry is a profound articulation of the strange dynamics of flourishing, an ancient precursor of the sentiments that Gibran would express so powerfully seven centuries later:

> *Sorrow prepares you for joy.*
> *It violently sweeps everything out of your house,*
> *So that new joy can find space to enter.*
> *It shakes the yellow leaves from the bough of your heart,*
> *So that fresh, green leaves can grow in their place.*[13]

For Rumi, the sorrow he felt over losing Shams became an almost rapturous state of spiritual yearning. And through his moving words we can see the final role of sadness: the *Poet of Melancholy*.

The Poet of Melancholy

The power of this final figure struck me with particular force one evening some years ago. I was in the Forrest Café, a cooperative in the heart of Edinburgh's Old Town. It served as a refuge for the strays of the city – pagans and punks mingling with artists and social workers – all drawn to its odd mix of reclaimed sofas, homemade food, experimental art shows and chaotic parties. I spent many a long night there during the nine beautiful years that I lived in the city. After graduating from Edinburgh University, I lingered there, living a dualistic existence. Half my time was spent working in the psychiatric hospital. The other half was devoted to my exciting but ultimately futile attempts to make it as a musician, my passion channelled into a sparky, soulful ska band. So I was often walking a tightrope – between the despair of the hospital and the excitement of band life.

I was in particularly dark spirits that evening. My shift in the hospital had been relentless and hard, sitting for hours with a deeply troubled patient. I was grateful for my freedom as I walked out into the cold night air, but I couldn't shake my melancholy. It wasn't just the sadness of the day weighing heavily on me, but a more pervasive sense of loneliness and failure. I was out of favour with love, ruing past mistakes and longing, in vain, for some sort of connection. Yearning for company, I trudged to the Forrest, hoping to see a familiar face. Reassuringly, an acoustic music night was in full swing, so I eased into a quiet corner and let myself be soothed by the gentle melodies of the duo on stage. After half an hour, I was woken from my reverie by someone in the audience requesting a rendition of 'Hallelujah', the heart-rending ballad by Leonard Cohen, the archetypal poet of melancholy.

The story of the genesis of 'Hallelujah' has become almost as legendary as the song itself. Bob Dylan once asked Cohen how long he took to write the song and was astounded when he replied, 'The best part of two years.' (In return, Cohen enquired about Dylan's 'I and I', and was equally astonished to hear that he had seemingly composed it in fifteen minutes.) Artists throughout the centuries – from poets like John Keats to painters like Vincent van Gogh – have delved deep into their personal sorrows to explore the ecstasy and heartache of love. But, for me, 'Hallelujah' is incomparable, particularly its apotheosis in the timeless cover by Jeff Buckley.

'Hallelujah' is a Hebrew word, meaning 'praise the Lord'. Cohen's hymn, though, is a paean to the divine, terrifying mystery of *love*. He bears witness to the way that love can both raise us to the heavens and leave us in despair. As C. S. Lewis wrote in *The Four Loves*, 'To love at all is to be vulnerable. Love anything and your heart will be wrung and possibly broken'.[14] Dwelling in the centre of love is sadness – a melancholic worry over its fragility, perhaps; or a quiet fear at the thought of losing it – which engenders its rich yet delicate texture. The crucial point, though, is that sadness is not an aberration of love, but the very condition of it, the levy to be paid in order to be in love. We must place our fate and happiness in the hands of an 'other' whose reciprocal love cannot be guaranteed and whose actions cannot be controlled. To be in love, we must accept this awesome risk, this transcendent blend of light and dark, with grace. In the words of Zygmunt Bauman, 'to love means opening up to that fate, that most sublime of all human conditions, one in which fear blends with joy into an alloy that no longer allows its ingredients to separate'.[15]

For Leonard Cohen, whatever fortune love holds for us, whatever sorrow and injury it may bring, we must continue to praise it, simply because there is no higher state on Earth. As such, seen through the eyes of the *Poet of Melancholy*, even the sadness within love can assume an ethereal beauty. Indeed, with this poetic sensibility, we might be able to transform all kinds of sadness – not only the melancholy within love – into fragments of beauty.

I felt this potent beauty for myself that evening in the Forrest. As the appeal for 'Hallelujah' rang out, not knowing the song well themselves, the musicians asked if anyone in the room could play it. Despite my dark mood – or perhaps because of it – I rose and walked to the stage. I like to think I channelled the supernatural power of Jeff Buckley and gave the performance of a lifetime, but in reality I no doubt warbled my way unsteadily through. Nevertheless, swept up in the moment, something in the room seemed to shift and I, for one, was certainly transported to another place. My sorrow burned like a flame. For a few minutes, I felt that everyone in the room was united, all hearts tender with the same hopes and fears. In this communion, we seemed to transcend mere sadness and it became almost a thing of beauty.

Indeed, this whole chapter has been a lyrical attempt to penetrate the surface gloom of sadness, not only to understand its value but to perceive its quiet, opaque aesthetics. As an expression of love and care, we have seen its power refracted across numerous qualities, from the protection of the *Medic of the Battlefield*, to the compassion of the *Angel of Sorrow*. Through these poetic devices, we can not only acknowledge the subtle power of sadness but are perhaps emboldened to befriend its different guises and appreciate their dignified presence in our lives.

And with that, we walk on, emerging from the vale of sadness with a refreshed, uplifted heart. Moreover, the benign reappraisal of sadness we have undertaken here may give us the strength to embark upon the next stage of our journey – onto the shaky path of anxiety. For we will find that, although anxiety can be troubling, it also plays a vital role in keeping our lives on track.

CHAPTER TWO

Anxiety

The path into the realm of anxiety is certainly rocky. Whereas sadness may be felt as a kind of heaviness, with anxiety we tend to feel an internal quickening – a fluttering, nervous agitation. While sadness slows our heartbeat down, anxiety hastens it, setting the pulse racing alarmingly. Despite their differences, though, the words 'sadness' and 'anxiety' both leap off the page laden with negative connotations. We invariably portray anxiety as an inherently 'bad thing'. Yet, just like sadness – and indeed all of the dark emotions that are discussed in this book – it may prove to be a surprising and resourceful ally in our quest to flourish and find fulfilment.

To set the tone, let's take a trip back to 1921. In a quiet corner of San Francisco, a psychologist named Lewis Terman was poring over the results of an extensive round of intelligence testing that had just been conducted in the city's schools. Fascinated by excellence, he wanted to know what made certain people stand out from the crowd, so he decided to gather as much data as possible on the fifteen hundred or so exceptionally bright eleven-year-olds who scored highest in the tests. These were the early years of the field of psychology, and there was much excitement around new-fangled questionnaires that purported to measure mysterious human qualities, such as personality. Hence, 1528 bright-eyed kids sat in their dusty classrooms, pencils in hands, answering questions that Terman believed would reveal the deepest aspects of their characters and the secrets of their success.

But this was only the start of Terman's grand project. He and his team continued to contact the children every few years to track their lives through the tumultuous decades of the twentieth century. Terman himself passed away in 1956, but his colleagues kept the research going, right until 1986, when the remaining 769 participants – now in the twilights of their own lives – were assessed for a final time. Terman's daring aim was to explore the extent to which factors that are present in childhood (such as personality) determine people's fates later in life – from social status and career success, to health and happiness. The results were striking. Childhood personality appeared to have a lasting legacy, affecting all aspects of life, including mortality.

In the early 1990s, a researcher named Howard Friedman returned to the original tests from 1921. He wanted to establish if any factors distinguished the long-lived group of survivors (who were still alive in 1986) from those who had passed away over the previous six and a half decades.[1] And, indeed, there were. Intriguingly, anxiety seemed to play a central role, but in a rather surprising way. At the time, the prevailing view among psychologists and doctors was that stress and anxiety took a heavy toll on the human body. As such, most of them recommended that people should try to reduce these burdens for the sake of their health, wellbeing and longevity. Indeed, in Terman's study, children who were highly worried and nervous in 1921 appeared to suffer ill health over subsequent years. Yet, Friedman's analysis revealed that the members of the original cohort with sunny, cheerful dispositions did not appear to be graced with any particular longevity, either. Rather, the key to a long life seemed to be *conscientiousness*: those who displayed a kind of anxious diligence – sometimes described as 'healthy neuroticism' – during childhood subsequently tended to enjoy longer, healthier lives than their peers.

Harnessing Anxiety

In speaking of the potential value of anxiety, we need to tread a similarly fine line to that taken in the previous chapter. There we saw how, if sadness crosses a certain line of severity and/or duration, it may turn into depression. Likewise, here we need to differentiate between 'healthy' and 'unhealthy' anxiety. As for where the line between these might be, I would again recommend following the American Psychiatric Association's guidelines, which are outlined in the Further Help and Resources section at the end of this book. Also, if you are worried that your anxiety is becoming unhealthy – perhaps if it is affecting your daily routine or seems to be constantly present – I would once again encourage you to consult your doctor, who will be able to offer you the appropriate guidance and support. Until the moment when anxiety becomes 'unhealthy', however, it can be very valuable and useful. Yet we often lose sight of this. Just as sadness is frequently swept up within the concept of depression and treated as inherently problematic, we are liable to condemn all forms of anxiety as dysfunctional.

Essentially, anxiety is our emotional risk antenna, sweeping our environment for threats. It has been honed by millions of years of evolutionary history to provide us with an inner radar which ensures that we are alert to phenomena that may harm us. From a Darwinian perspective, this is a good thing – not merely beneficial, but essential to our survival. Otherwise, we would ignore the approaching sabretoothed tiger and become its lunch. Of course, this radar may 'malfunction' from time to time. It may be hyper-vigilant, operating on a hair trigger. Or it may provide justifiable warnings, but its frantic clamouring is out of all proportion to the severity of the threat or the likelihood of its occurrence. Or the alarm may continue to sound remorselessly, even once the threat has receded. If any of these problems persist, that may be a sign that a person's anxiety has become unhealthy, and could be regarded as a disorder. But when it's working well, anxiety performs various functions that are vital for our safety and prosperity.

To get a sense of these functions, let's imagine an ancient community living in relative isolation. A sense of impending crisis – say, a shortage of food – compels the villagers to assemble an elite team who will venture out in search of a solution. Each recruit is chosen for their ability to provide an essential skill upon which the success of the mission will depend. First, there is the *Prophet*, a perceptive seer who was the first to see the village's perilous situation, and recognise the need to address it. Second, the *Trainer*, who is responsible for advance planning and preparation. Third, the *Motivator*, an enthusiastic cheerleader who cajoles the team into action and drives it forward. Fourth, the *Lookout*, the vigilant eyes and ears of the group, on guard for immanent threat. Finally, leading boldly from the front, is the trailblazing *Pioneer*, who fearlessly guides the squad into uncharted territory. Together, these five symbolic figures personify the qualities and skills relating to anxiety that we can draw on as we make our way through life.

The Prophet

The first key character is the observant, vigilant outrider who first notices that something is amiss. While everyone else merrily goes about their business as usual, the *Prophet* realises that food supplies are dwindling, storm clouds are gathering on the horizon and subtle changes in the air signify an impending crisis. And so it is with our mind: anxiety is our siren, alerting us to dangers that may lie ahead. Indeed, humans are equipped with a *dual* alarm system – an arsenal featuring both anxiety and fear.[2] The difference between the two is mainly temporal. Fear is an urgent warning of *present* danger, motivating us into immediate action. In contrast, anxiety is a searchlight that probes the dark, hazy realm of the *future*, picking out potential problems that might come to pass. Hence, anxiety is more diffuse and less specific than fear. We may not be able to pin down the source of our concern, and even if we can, its unpredictability means that it is difficult to know if we should pay attention to it or not. Nevertheless, by alerting us to potential calamities, anxiety serves the valuable function of prompting us to take action to avert disaster, or at least prepare for it and lessen its impact.

Fans of the spectacular *Game of Thrones* will be familiar with Jon Snow's dark warnings about the menace beyond the wall. Perhaps it's something in the name, for in 1854 a distant namesake presciently sounded the alarm for a very real crisis that was unfolding on the dank, cobblestoned streets of Victorian London. All around, the deadly threat of cholera hung in the air – a vicious intestinal infection that was ravaging England's cramped capital, leaving thousands of corpses in its wake. At the time, it was believed that this plague was spread through a vaguely defined, sulphurous 'miasma', a ghostlike poison that suffused the fetid air. However, amid the general panic, a young anaesthesiologist named John Snow embarked upon a remarkable act of prognostication that would eventually save thousands of lives in London, and then millions of lives around the world, through the changes to public health practices that he inspired. A real-life medical Sherlock Holmes (or indeed Gregory House MD, for fans of Hugh Laurie), Snow intuitively suspected that cholera was actually spread through contaminated water. This was his crucial gift: being able to see what no one else could perceive. Yet, his foresight might well have gone unheeded if he had not then engaged in a daring act of empiricism that essentially founded the field of epidemiology (the study of the spread of disease).

Ingeniously, Snow decided to map the epidemic – an exercise that was far more revolutionary and courageous in the 1850s than it sounds today. He lived in Soho, at that time a squalid mess of drinking dens and slaughterhouses, where a particularly brutal outbreak of cholera was unfolding right on his doorstep. Keeping his cool amid his neighbours' panic, he was determined to prove that the disease could be traced back to a single contaminated water source. Bravely – given the widespread belief that the infection was transmitted through the air – he visited the homes of those who had perished and interviewed their grieving families. In doing so, he discovered that every death had occurred within the vicinity of one water pump – on the corner of Broad Street and Cambridge Street. Snow's quarry was in sight. Being a good scientist, though, he sought further proof. He examined a sample of water from the pump, and sure enough it contained the deadly microbial traces of cholera. Armed with this discovery, he pleaded with the local authority to shut down the pump, and they finally agreed to do so despite considerable scepticism. The outbreak ceased almost immediately.

Snow's investigation led directly to the safe water and sewage systems that billions of people around the world use today. It is thanks to him, and other medical pioneers like him, that many of the epidemiological horrors of past generations are thankfully confined to history.

Sadly, though, other *Prophets* have been fated to be modern-day Cassandras. (Apollo bestowed the power of foresight on Cassandra, but then, after she had refused his attempts at seduction, made her suffer the torment that none of her predictions were believed.) One such figure is the formidable Brooksley Born, a former chair of the Commodity Futures Trading Commission, the US agency that monitors the arcane world of commodities trading. Soon after taking up this role in 1994, Born realised that an entire realm under her jurisdiction – the market in fiendishly complex financial instruments known as derivatives – was shrouded in darkness. It was an unregulated 'black box' of esoteric transactions that few people understood. Worse still, the sums of money that were cascading through these secretive channels were staggering. By 2007, on the eve of the crash, the derivatives market was valued at a mind-blowing $595 trillion, with the underlying securities (the value of the deposits at risk) worth a frightening $3.2 trillion.

With dread, in the late 1990s Born correctly predicted that the implosion of this market would unleash a tsunami of defaults and losses that could capsize the world economy. As it continued to career out of control, she implored the authorities to mend the system before catastrophe struck. But they did not seem to hear her, and indeed gave the impression of not *wanting* to listen. Under sustained pressure from thousands of financial lobbyists, the US Congress went so far as to pass legislation prohibiting Born's agency from regulating the derivatives market. Infuriated and frustrated, she resigned in 1999, joining a long list of Cassandras whose frantic alarm bells have been ignored or drowned out by louder voices.

So, the first lesson here is: if the *Prophet* speaks – if you hear warning bells sounding inside you, however faintly – pay attention and listen. Upon further investigation, it may turn out to be a false alarm, in which case you can rest easy. But our antenna for trouble is usually fairly sensitive and reliable, so the warning may well need to be heeded and acted upon. This point is key: prophets serve no purpose if their warnings are ignored. So, if our antenna picks up a sign of trouble, we should take action. Otherwise, anxiety just chases its own tail, round and round in a vicious downward spiral of worry and fear. To be of use, anxiety must engender corrective efforts to tackle its source. So, once our inner *Prophet* has identified a potential problem, looming on the horizon, we must prepare for its impending arrival. With this, we come to the *Trainer*.

The Trainer

It is May 2001, and Chris Hadfield is about to do something he has dreamed about all his life, and which only a handful of people have ever had the terrifying privilege to experience: a spacewalk. Up in the cold, lonely vastness, he eases himself out of the hatch of the International Space Station. This fragile miracle of human engineering is orbiting some 270 miles above the earth at 17,500 miles an hour. And Hadfield is clinging to the outside, all but face-to-face with God. Not only that, he has the dazzlingly delicate job of installing a multimillion-dollar piece of machinery – a new robotic arm. After five long hours, immersed in his task, he notices something troubling. Some droplets of moisture have appeared, as if from nowhere, and are floating ominously around the inside of his helmet. Then, suddenly – *bang* – his left eye begins to sting as one of the droplets enters it. The pain is vicious, but with no gravity to dislodge the liquid, Hadfield's eye quickly begins to cloud with tears, which also have no means of escape. Before long, he is unsighted in his left eye. Then his salty tears start migrating across the bridge of his nose, making their way to his good right eye. Soon, he is effectively blind. Knowing that the brightest minds in North America are intensely following his every move back on Earth, with preternatural sangfroid he paraphrases the immortal line: 'Houston . . . we have a problem.'

This scenario would probably leave most mortals paralysed with fear. But in his remarkable autobiography,[3] Hadfield explains that the rigorous NASA training enabled both himself and the ground crew to remain relatively calm while they methodically performed some high-wire diagnostic and problem-solving gymnastics. Crucially, Hadfield and his colleagues were able to circumvent the debilitating fear that most of us would feel in such a precarious situation because they had endured extreme anxiety in advance and had learned how to work through it. He describes how NASA trainers would put the budding astronauts through endless 'bad news' simulations, covering all manner of potentially deadly emergencies – from a fire to an outbreak of illness. These intensive preparations, which essentially involved a pre-emptive collective harnessing of anxiety, meant that the astronauts were better able to handle any real adversity that might occur. As Hadfield writes, 'Being forced to confront the problem of failure head-on – to study it, dissect it, tease apart all its components and consequences – really works. After a few years of doing that pretty much daily you've forged the strongest possible armor to defend against fear: hard-won competence.' True, sudden blindness on a spacewalk had never been addressed in the training. But that training did allow Hadfield to remain cool under pressure as he and the ground crew worked out a solution. (He opened a valve in the helmet and the droplets disappeared into space.) With his sight restored, he calmly returned to his task and installed the robotic arm.

Chris Hadfield is thus a passionate and articulate advocate for the 'positive power of negative thinking'; and not only in the rarefied atmosphere of space, but when facing all of life's challenges. He perceptively takes aim at voguish 'positive thinking' techniques – those fist-pumping 'visualise success' strategies that you might expect to hear from a slick corporate trainer. You may well ask, 'What's so wrong with anticipating your dream outcome when you face a serious challenge?' For instance, perhaps the mere thought of an upcoming job interview causes you to break out in a cold sweat. So wouldn't it be better to picture the interview panel offering you the job on the spot and then applauding you out of the interview room? Such fantasies may be delicious to indulge. However, in the cold light of day we are far better served by tuning into and harnessing our anxieties.

Hence, the second member of our metaphorical team is the *Trainer*. Having listened to the *Prophet*'s perceptive warnings, the *Trainer* organises practice routines and contingency plans to enable us to deal with potential mishaps. Like a field marshal preparing his troops assiduously for battle, or a football coach diligently studying his next opponents, we have much to gain from proactive, anxiety-fuelled preparation for anything that life may throw at us.

Take that job interview, for example – one of life's more common anxiety-laden events. As the all-important day looms, most of us feel increasingly frequent pangs of worry. Your inner *Prophet* will be issuing warnings about possible missteps – from arriving late and dishevelled, to tripping over your words. But this is a good thing, because it means your risk antenna has alerted you to possible problems ahead of time. At this point, the *Trainer* can step forward and implement preparatory actions to mitigate these threats.

Anxious about arriving late? OK, that is a legitimate concern, but we can do something about it. Let's factor in an extra hour for the journey, and trace the route in advance. Worried about freezing under questioning? Let's identify some likely questions and rehearse key responses that will impress the panel. I saw the power of this technique myself when I had an interview that represented a real game-changer for me, career wise. I had almost no expectation of getting the job, as it was a huge step up. Nevertheless, for several days beforehand, I practised responses that I thought would make me shine. I continued to rehearse them right up to the last moment, like a nervous actor just before the curtain rises. And it worked: against the odds, I got the job.

So, if anxiety calls, listen and heed its advice. Use it skilfully in the service of preparation that will increase the likelihood of achieving your goals, whatever they may be. But anxiety's role does not end there. Our next figure shows the crucial role that it can play in pushing us to reach those goals.

The Motivator

You may have heard fevered tales of *The Secret*. Perched tantalisingly on the self-help shelves, this wildfire bestseller makes a promise that seems too good to be true: ask and you shall receive. The universe is painted as a celestial Aladdin's lamp ... or, to use a more apt metaphor, a giant mail-order service. The book's beguiling notion is that we need only visualise our heart's desires and by some mysterious 'law of attraction' the universe will oblige and send them our way. The appeal of this wish-fulfilment dream is understandable, and arguably the same impulse that underpins religious petitionary prayer ('God, please grant me ... ').

Sadly, it probably *is* too good to be true. In fact, a fascinating series of studies has suggested that this type of positive visualisation may even be counter-productive and push our dreams further out of reach.[4] It seems that visualisations of success can seductively lull the mind into believing, on some level, that the prize is already in the bag. Hence, we ease up and start to celebrate before we are even close to crossing the line. Conversely, when we are worried that an outcome is in doubt, when we fear that an elusive but longed-for reward will be snatched from our grasp, we continue to fight hard, reach high, move fast. So, once we've realised the necessity of the mission (courtesy of the *Prophet*) and have made meticulous preparations (thanks to the *Trainer*), we need to call upon the *Motivator* – the cheerleader who rallies the troops and propels the mission forward.

To succeed, we need to have faith in our own talent and believe in at least the possibility of success. But it is far better for this self-confidence to be anxious and concerned, rather than laid-back and complacent. This negative edge drives people towards the extraordinary levels of commitment that are required to attain the most elusive goals. Consider one of the true legends of modern sport, David Beckham. While his iconic status is no doubt due in part to his matinee-idol looks and good-natured charm, it is worth remembering that he won a record 115 caps for England because of his footballing ability. Such achievements are possible only by allying natural talent with utter dedication. In Beckham's case, he put in the kind of relentless practice that is only possible if your inner *Motivator* urges you to keep going for one more session, one more hour, one more day, year after year. As a child, he perhaps had peers who were more naturally gifted footballers. But he would spend hour after hour in the park with his father – long into the dark of the evening – endlessly practising the free kicks for which he would eventually become world famous. His rise to the pinnacle of his sport is testament to a passionate quest for perfection. He never succumbed to complacency, and nor should we, as we strive towards our own summits of achievement, whatever they may be.

Away from the exemplary determination of heroes like Beckham, Heather Kappes and Gabriele Oettingen neatly captured the value of anxiety as a powerful motivating force in a series of imaginative experiments. Their studies form part of the scientific world's response to *The Secret*, and they were able to demonstrate a kind of *anti*-law of attraction. In one study, Kappes and Oettingen asked one group of students to fantasise about a positive week ahead, brimming with personal and academic success, and another group to visualise it in whatever way came to mind.[5] Seven days later, all of the participants reported back on their week's accomplishments. It transpired that the first group had achieved far less than the second. It was as if, without the jolt of anxiety, their motors never really got running. In a second study two years later, the same researchers found that fantasising about the positive resolution of a major crisis – such as starvation in Africa – had a negative impact on philanthropy. Envisioning the eventual success of a project seemed to dampen people's willingness to offer large amounts of money, time or effort to the cause.[6] These insidious effects of positive fantasies were not limited to laboratory experiments. In a third study, Kappes and Oettingen looked at a remedial vocational course for students from socio-economically disadvantaged backgrounds.[7] Contrary to the course organisers' expectations, those students who pictured bright, rosy futures for themselves because of their participation in the scheme had worse attendance records and ultimately achieved lower grades than their more negative counterparts.

This doesn't mean that we should belittle such initiatives and their goals. But it may be wise to combine optimism with mild concern, rather than portray them as guaranteed routes to success. Indeed, Kappes and Oettingen have devised a technique to facilitate just this kind of delicate balancing act, which they call 'mental contrasting'. This involves systematically alternating between positive and negative thoughts about the future: a pleasant daydream here; a nervous worry there. Mental contrasting appears to be an effective means to promote long-term behavioural change, as was seen, for instance, in a therapeutic intervention that was devised to promote healthy eating.[8] A judicious mixture of hope (about being on a healthier life track) and anxiety (about falling off that track) seemed to be just what the participants needed to prod their incalcitrant bodies and minds in the right direction. And the best internal *Motivators* will provide precisely that beneficial combination: inspiring us through hope and positivity, while driving us forward through concern and worry.

The mission is well under way, now that the *Motivator* is driving the team along. But to ensure we remain vigilant to new threats that may emerge along the way, we need to call upon the fourth member of our squadron – the *Lookout*.

The Lookout

The *Lookout* is the eyes and ears of the mission, the figure who guarantees the group's safe passage to its destination. Here, we are talking about anxiety as our cautious, vigilant eye, scanning the environment for immanent signs of danger (as opposed to the *Prophet*, whose warnings are based on an intuitive understanding of the threats that may lie ahead). I picture this sentinel as a hardy, solitary figure, braving the elements alone, a guardian angel who keeps watch while everyone else is fast asleep.

Indeed, when I think about the *Lookout*, my mind always turns to the haunting tale of the *Titanic*. I wonder why, over a century on, this tragedy still captivates the world's imagination. One reason, perhaps, is that the calamity was so nearly averted. Reverberating down the decades are the stories of numerous perceptive and diligent *Lookouts* who tried to warn of the impending catastrophe, but whose cries went unheeded. Even before the doomed liner set sail, Maurice Clarke, the safety inspector, warned the White Star Line that it would need at least 50 per cent more life boats.[9] Scandalously, Clarke was reportedly told to keep quiet, or face the sack. Then there was Cyril Evans, the telegraph operator on the SS *California*, which was making her own lonely voyage across the Atlantic on that dark night in April 1912. Sighting icebergs, the *California*'s captain told Evans to notify other vessels, which he did. Tragically, though, since the *California* was so close to the *Titanic*, Evans's warning blasted noisily through the headset of Jack Phillips – the *Titanic*'s wireless operator – while he was trying to listen to another call. So the alarm was never heard. And, of course, there was twenty-four-year-old Frederick Fleet, perched high up in the crow's nest as midnight approached, the liner's designated watchman at the fateful hour. Straining to see out over the calm water, under a frozen, moonless sky – meteorological factors that made his task particularly difficult – Fleet was the first to spot the looming iceberg. Frantically, he rang the bridge, but his warning came too late for the ship to change course. A few hours later, 1517 souls on board would be dead.

Epochal events like the sinking of the *Titanic* highlight the importance of heeding those who keep watch over us. Indeed, we can all probably find examples closer to home in which we've benefited from listening to the advice of an anxious *Lookout*. For instance, when I was six, my parents enrolled me in a local youth group called the Woodcraft Folk. Essentially, it was a kind of hippy, socialist version of the Scouts ... if you can imagine such a thing. It mingled left-wing solidarity and pacifism with Native American-inspired reverence for nature. There were also more prosaic activities, such as a fierce footballing rivalry with the Boys' Brigade (we were better!) and, in my later teenage years, drunken sing-songs around the campfire during our regular weekend trips to the countryside. I loved those adventures away from home. Apart from the occasional hazard – from the perpetual downpours of the British summer, to getting lost in the woods – they were magical trips.

Strangely, though, among my most vivid memories of that time is a rather daunting figure called Maurice. I believe that his children had attended the group way back when, before drifting away upon reaching adulthood. But Maurice himself had stayed on as one of a small group of idealistic leaders. He was a hardy outdoorsman – pretty gruff and a little fearsome – but he cared passionately about doing things right, about the 'spirit of Woodcraft', and above all about our welfare. He also had a talent for education, teaching *us* to care. His vigilance was constant. His eagle eyes could spot a poorly constructed tent a mile off, and he always seemed to know when rain was imminent. He would materialise from nowhere to tell us to pack away our belongings or to reprimand a child who was running carelessly in the kitchen tent. For me, he was the embodiment of one of the most evocative literary figures, the Catcher in the Rye, from J. D. Salinger's book of the same name. The novel's central character, Holden Caulfield, is asked what he wants to be when he grows up. All that comes to Holden's mind is an image of a vast field of rye, bordered by a sheer cliff, upon which countless children are playing. He finally replies that his dearest wish – his vocation in life – is simply to patrol the border of the field and gently prevent any children from falling over the edge. Although Holden is a troubled soul, and not someone we should necessarily seek to emulate, I've always found this image very powerful and inspiring. Looking back, Maurice was just such a figure, watching out for hundreds of clumsy, clueless kids, trying to steer us on the right path.

Naturally, I didn't always appreciate his vigilance at the time, and throughout my early teens I was mildly terrified that I would become the focus of his admonitions. But as I grew older, I started to see the respect in which he was held by other adults, and I began to recognise the value of his attention, and the wisdom of his guidance. He passed away when I was still young, collapsing while roaming across the mountains he loved so much. But his memory has stayed with me, as has the importance of his protective caution. I don't always live up to it – far from it! My life has been littered with foolish scrapes and close calls. But when I'm at my best, I do still try to follow his example. For I've increasingly come to appreciate that his kind of cautious anxiety is vital to our wellbeing, guarding us against danger. We can all channel our inner Maurice by remaining observant, looking around vigilantly, gently changing our path when necessary. Just as he kept watch over the kids running around the campsite, we can become our *own* Catcher in the Rye. This doesn't mean that we must stop living life to the full. It just means that we should do so with a degree of vigilance and prudence.

Let's take a practical example. Like many people, I find few thoughts more alluring and exhilarating than the idea of packing my bags and spiriting myself away across the ocean, expanding my world both literally and metaphorically. The trouble is, I'm a really anxious traveller. Much of this anxiety stems from previous troubles I've had on my wanderings, so it has some basis in reason and precedent. But now I try to use these worries to smooth my passage, and make it safer, by being extra vigilant and cautious about potential hazards. I once had my wallet stolen in Spain, which contained all the hard-won rewards of half a day's busking. So now I'm extra careful about how I carry my valuables, concealing them well, and keep a keen eye out for pickpockets. I had a close call in China, when, after drinking with a group of random locals, I found myself barricaded in a karaoke bar at 4 a.m., with the proprietors demanding all my money. So, now I'm rather more wary about traipsing off with strangers, at least until I've reassured myself that they are decent people. I once missed a train because I was daydreaming while on the Tube towards King's Cross. So, now I always try to remain attentive while I'm on the move.

The point is, anxiety doesn't have to be a dour killjoy, ruling out all playfulness and fun. The *Lookout* doesn't quash the possibility of adventure. It just means we approach it with a bit more wisdom and prudence. Take our astronaut friend Chris Hadfield. Strapping yourself into a Space Shuttle, powered by exploding booster rockets, each packing around 3 million pounds of thrust – 'riding a missile', as he puts it – is about as dangerous an activity as a human being can undertake. Yet, Hadfield describes himself as risk-*averse*. In reality, this means that he has appraised and calculated the risks, and has availed himself of all the necessary training to mitigate them. Having done so, he is empowered to buckle up and enjoy the ride. We should let our own anxiety do the same for us. Then we will come to realise that anxiety does not inhibit us from living a rich, exciting life; on the contrary, it makes such a life much more likely and attainable.

With this thought in mind, we come to the most elevated role that anxiety plays in our lives: the *Pioneer*.

The Pioneer

With the seemingly paradoxical example of Chris Hadfield – the risk-averse adventurer, cautiously undertaking a highly dangerous endeavour – we saw that, rather than a shackle that bolts us to the ground, anxiety enables life to be a bold, exhilarating ride, and allows us to survive long enough to enjoy it. Indeed, anxiety is arguably the very expression of humanity's pioneer spirit, the relentless quest for innovation that has propelled us all the way to the moon. It can be a glorious sign that we are testing our limits, striking out on new paths, climbing higher peaks. For, in those situations, it's only *natural* to feel anxious, because the ground is untrodden, uncertain, unpredictable. So, if you ever feel anxious, rather than viewing it as a flaw or a sign of failure, try to see it as a life-affirming indication that you are boldly pushing beyond your boundaries and embracing new challenges. This may entail riding a rocket into space or simply having the courage to introduce yourself to a stranger at a bar. The principle is exactly the same. Your sense of anxiety means that you are bravely stepping out of your comfort zone, and this is the only way people ever learn, grow and develop.

I experienced this myself when I embarked upon an adventure that, in hindsight, I can't quite believe I ever undertook. Encouraged by my mum, and prompted by the relationship break-up described in the previous chapter, at the age of nineteen I signed up to teach English in China. Looking back, I was barely out of adolescence. I know that many people have performed far braver and more radical deeds at younger ages than nineteen, but for me this was *way* out of my comfort zone. Friends had often ridiculed me for my lack of streetwise skills, my poor navigational ability – I always struggled to locate countries on a map – and generally for drifting by in a haze. So they were genuinely shocked when I announced that I was catapulting myself halfway round the world ... which was partly why I wanted to do it – to show them! It was a massive shock for me, too, though.

Just about every aspect of the trip was nerve-shredding. I was living abroad for the first time, standing in front of sixty

teenagers every day, trying my best to do a decent approxima-
tion of a teacher. I hauled myself around that vast, mysterious
land on my own, relying on my rudimentary Mandarin and
the kindness of bemused strangers. So, of course I was anxious,
all the time. I was testing myself – my nascent teaching skills,
my physical and emotional limits, my capacity for resilience
and adaptability – to the limit. I was constantly unsure, perpet-
ually out of my depth, invariably struggling. And yet – *for this
very reason* – my time in China transformed my life. I crossed so
many thresholds, surpassed my own expectations in so many
ways, found my feet as a human being, and returned home a
new person. As the challenges continued to unfold, I began to
see my anxiety as a sign that I was breaking down *self-imposed*
barriers and ascending into uncharted territory.

This rejuvenating idea of anxiety as the mark of a *Pioneer*
is seen most forcefully in the bracing work of the existen-
tialists. Even their names seem to capture this bold spirit.
They are redolent of imposing mountain peaks – Heidegger,
Kierkegaard – or courageous resistance fighters – Sartre,
Camus. These philosophers were all bound by a common
concern with exploring the 'human condition', and, in their
individual ways, they all took a keen interest in anxiety.
Moreover, they would all probably agree with the idea that
anxiety is the very condition of embracing life, the 'price
tag' of living boldly and fully. Consider, for example, Søren
Kierkegaard, the Danish theologian who is regarded as the
father of existentialism. In his influential 1844 classic *The
Concept of Anxiety*, he argued that 'Whoever has learned to
be anxious in the right way has learned the ultimate.'[10] What
might this mysterious sentence mean? I'm wary of trying to
capture a philosophy as nuanced and subtle as Kierkegaard's

in a few short sentences. But it is probably fair to say that he took an almost metaphysical view of anxiety, which he understood to be the *feeling* of freedom. In his words, 'anxiety is freedom's possibility'. Living life to the full means being aware of the almost infinite array of possibilities that lie before us – the forks in the road, the countless choices that must be made, from the insignificant to the life-defining – and then choosing wisely and decisively.

Each and every decision takes us down one road, and leaves others untravelled. It is only natural that we feel anxious about the consequences of our choices. But this is life! It can't be helped, and the only way to avoid such worry is to decline to undertake the journey at all, which essentially means refusing to live. So, as we feel anxiety rising, we could try to view it as our existential validation. It is a visceral sign that we are *really* living, grasping life's possibilities, plunging headlong into opportunity. As Kierkegaard put it, 'Anxiety is the dizziness of freedom, the awareness of the possibility of being able'.[11] Consequently, as we start to understand the various roles that anxiety plays in our lives – the *Prophet* who foresees potential troubles ahead, the *Trainer* who prepares us for the journey, the *Motivator* who keeps us driven, the *Lookout* who stays alert and finally the *Pioneer* who boldly strikes forth into new territory – we can truly appreciate the intricate ways in which it helps us flourish.

With that, we leave behind the rocky road of anxiety and venture into the desert heat of anger. These two share a kinship, in that both are expressions of concern when something is amiss in our world. But whereas we should heed anxiety's warnings, we can harness anger's energy to shape our world for the better, as the next chapter explains.

CHAPTER THREE

Anger

Consider this scenario. You turn on the news, and there, dressed resplendently in an expensive suit, stands a new MP, fresh on the political scene after a lucrative business career. Smiling out through the screen, he announces a bold new initiative: baby auctions. For too long, he declares, the arenas of human love and procreation have been excluded from 'market forces'. The time has come to bring the profit motive into the production of children and finally allow people their long-denied right to cash in by selling their progeny to the highest bidder. How would you feel? Totally appalled and brewing with anger, I would imagine.

Philip Tetlock and his colleagues encountered exactly those reactions when they posed this horrendous idea – and other 'taboo' scenarios – to a wide-eyed panel of volunteers, who were no doubt left wondering which sinister dimension of reality they had stumbled into.[1] Right across the political spectrum, from socialists to conservatives, every one of the participants in the experiment expressed outrage at this crass violation of the sanctity of love and the dignity of human beings, in recognition that some things are sacred and must remain above the grubby realm of commerce. Moreover, they were all so disgusted that they vowed to engage in some form of 'moral cleansing' – as if they felt dirty for even contemplating the above scenario – such as joining an anti-baby-auction campaign.

As disquieting as such experiments may be, they highlight an important and even redemptive idea: anger can be a *moral* emotion. Not always, admittedly: sometimes it is simply the irruption of destructive aggression, with no justification or value. But, just as we (hopefully) learn to defuse our irrational, violent impulses through experience and maturity, so we can begin to recognise when our anger might be a moral signal – a visceral response to someone crossing a line, breaching an ethic.

This interpretation of anger has somewhat fallen out of favour lately. In Chapter 1 we saw the unfortunate trend for sadness to be subsumed within the umbrella concept of depression, and the medical fraternity's increasing inclination to treat it as a mild form of the disorder. Similarly, anger is frequently painted in judgemental tones as a dysfunctional and dangerous emotional state. True enough, often it is that. As such, we shall be alert in this chapter to forms of anger that constitute nothing more than destructive aggression, and therefore need to be controlled and muted. But we shall also see that, if listened to carefully and used skilfully, anger may sometimes act as a moral compass that can direct us towards a brighter future. As the great progressive movements of recent years – from feminism to civil rights – have shown, a sense of *righteous* anger can inspire social change and ultimately create a more just society. Even if such change is slow to manifest, and the struggle can seem never-ending, there is value in the solidarity we feel when joining a campaign, working with others in the service of a higher ideal. Moreover, rewards can accrue even if we take a stand alone. There can be dignity and worth in staying true to a meaningful value, and living rightfully by it.

Disentangling Anger, Frustration, Aggression and Hate

There is a pivotal phrase in the previous paragraph: 'if listened to carefully and used skilfully'. We must tread cautiously, because engaging with anger is rather like kindling a fire: it is a potent force, and while it can be useful if channelled well, it is more often chaotic and destructive, and you might be the one who suffers most. Try to bring to mind the last time you felt angry. This might have been provoked by something deeply wounding, like a loved one's betrayal. Or it might have been sparked by something far more prosaic, such as the sheer frustration of being stuck in an interminable traffic jam, or your computer crashing, wiping away hours of work. Right across this broad spectrum of provocations, the anger itself generally feels the same, at least at first. It ignites as a spark of rage, bubbling up inside with great energy – an explosive force, yearning for vengeance and ready to burst forth with violence.

To return to our key phrase – 'if listened to carefully and used skilfully' – the examples above contain two key lessons. First, it should be remembered that not all anger is moral.

Sometimes we get angry simply because life isn't going our way, and we feel our desires are being thwarted. In such cases, it is probably more accurate to speak of *frustration*, rather than anger. This is the prickly irritation we feel when we're stuck and seemingly helpless, be it in the face of an unending traffic jam or an uncooperative laptop. Like a child, we stomp our feet as if the universe might be shaken into an arrangement that is more aligned with our needs. That said, even though this frustration is not a moral emotion, we can still learn from it. Our annoyance in a traffic jam may, on reflection, generate some useful insights. For instance, it may lead to a realisation that we are overstressed, and prompt us to make some significant life changes. It may embarrass us into admitting that we lack patience and acceptance, and cause us to join a meditation class in order to cultivate those valuable qualities. It may encourage us to rethink our commutes and travel by a different route. But we should never lose sight of the fact that such frustrations are really only minor irritations, and their resolution should not be equated with a moral crusade. Viewing them as anything more than that does a disservice to those moments when anger truly is a moral issue.

The second lesson is even more important. When anger begins to froth and simmer with explosive potential, it is essential to use this energy skilfully and channel it towards making life better. This demands deliberation and care. No one is well served, least of all yourself, by lashing out aggressively in an unthinking, reactive way. Crude anger, if unwisely directed, can all too easily degenerate into the raging of our inner thug. Sure, there may be a moral kernel in there somewhere, but even this noble impulse can become polluted by self-interest and hijacked by latent aggression.

Just as our character contains many wonderful elements – as illustrated throughout this book – it also harbours more regrettable impulses, inner demons that agitate for destruction, violence and hate. We must guard against these elements seizing hold of justified anger and co-opting it for their hostile ends. If this is allowed to happen, the anger's energy may turn into a hateful fire that can consume you and lay waste to everyone around you, indiscriminately and wantonly. No one wins in that situation, especially not you. As the Buddha put it, 'Holding on to anger is like grasping a hot coal with the intent of throwing it at someone else; you are the one who gets burned'.[2]

Harnessing Anger

In light of the Buddha's warning, this chapter will explain how to harness anger skilfully and wisely. We all know that this is a difficult task. As Aristotle said, over two millennia ago, 'Anybody can become angry – that is easy, but to be angry with the right person and to the right degree and at the right time and for the right purpose, and in the right way – that is not within everybody's power and is not easy'.[3] But at the risk of disagreeing with the venerable philosopher, most of us can, with considered reflection, learn to use anger's energy to propel us forward in positive ways.

Most of us have felt betrayed at one time or another by a loved one or a close acquaintance. Perhaps you are still in contact with the person who hurt you – be it a cheating partner or an unreliable friend or a disloyal colleague. In that case, your anger might stimulate an eloquent assertion of your rights in which you clarify that you deserve and demand better treatment. On the other hand, perhaps the hurtful person is now a spectral figure, tormenting you from the unreachable shadows of the past, such as a parent who mistreated you as a child but has since passed away. In that case, your anger could form part of your moral compass. Knowing the harm the person wreaked, you might make it your life's mission to refute their misdeeds. Let your anger drive you to be the best, most loving person you can be. Use it to become everything that they were not.

To see how anger might be used to address these iniquities skilfully, let us think about how a crime might be successfully redressed. First, a *Watchful Citizen* might witness the misdeed itself. Then a *Sharp-eyed Detective* will set about gathering evidence, before a *Discerning Police Officer* identifies and arrests the miscreant. In court, an *Eloquent Prosecutor* assembles a rigorous case against the offender, which a *Merciful Juror* considers carefully, remaining fair and reasonable throughout the trial. A *Wise Judge* dispenses justice once the verdict has been reached, setting an appropriate sentence according to their insightful interpretation of the law. Finally, a *Reforming Prison Governor* metes out any corrective punishment deemed necessary, but the primary goal will remain rehabilitation rather than retribution.

The Watchful Citizen

Picture yourself in a rowing boat on a river. You and your family are enjoying a tranquil day on the water, drifting languidly downstream. Of course, you are watchful, vigilant.

As we saw in the previous chapter, we must always remain alert to possible threats if we are to live life to the full. And one such threat duly appears. Your reverie is brusquely interrupted by an aggressively blaring horn. You sit bolt upright and see, heading straight towards you, a hulking barge. Although moving sedately, its advance is unrelenting. Hence the horn – the skipper evidently expects you to make the necessary evasive manoeuvres. But you can't because your boat is heavy and cumbersome. By contrast, the barge's skipper could easily put his vessel's powerful motor into reverse and ease to a halt. Yet still it bears down on you and your family, and your concern escalates into panic. You wave in a bid to catch the skipper's attention, but to no avail; he is hidden from view. As the barge edges ever closer, you brace yourself for impact. The crash shunts your boat violently into the riverbank.

Your first reaction, after anxiously checking that everyone is unhurt, is a flame of heated anger. How could the skipper have disregarded your safety so callously? This initial burst of rage is an internal warning light, a sign that we may have suffered mistreatment. Only possibly, though. Even as the blood rises, most of us would not immediately leap on board the barge and ball our fists in readiness to pummel the skipper. Sure, we might be fizzing with indignation, but this is usually overridden by a sense of confusion, and an urgent need for answers. *Why* did the barge crash into us? You clamber over to the vessel, which has crashed into the bank a few yards downstream. A number of scenarios now pass through your mind. What if the barge is empty? There was no skipper, just a boat that had slipped free of its moorings. Or, if there is a skipper, has he been frantically wrestling with a broken throttle? Or he is lying prone on deck, having suffered a heart attack? What happens to our anger then?

Our tendency to assume that someone is at fault is known in psychology as the 'fundamental attribution error'.[4] Most of the time, we attribute a person's behaviour to their personal disposition and fail to recognise any mitigating situational factors. For instance, say your boss walks past you in a corridor and ignores your cheerful hello. You may well leap to the conclusion that he dislikes you and doesn't appreciate your hard work. Few of us would entertain the possibility that he is just having a terrible day and didn't see us because he was preoccupied with worry. Or say a friend fails to attend your party. Either they are an awful person who can't be bothered to trek across town, or you are an awful person who must have done something dreadful to warrant the cold shoulder. Far more reasonable situational explanations – such as that they never received the invitation or they had to work late – are usually overlooked. Or say a driver cuts you up at a junction. Clearly, he is an ogre who is selfishly ploughing his way home, rather than a frazzled parent who is rushing his sick child to hospital. Such apparent 'injustices' raise our hackles almost every time and ignite the indignation of anger. But when we learn the mitigating factors, our anger dissipates immediately, like a punctured balloon.

In each of our three alternative potential barge scenarios, the anger would suddenly evaporate, to be replaced by a sense of concern. No one is to blame; no aggressor deserves our ire. The accident was just one of those things, unforeseeable and unpreventable. So, if we feel rage starting to bubble up, our first duty is to be cautious and remember that not all hurts are intentional, so not all anger is moral. Before we get into the business of using anger skilfully, we must first accept that it is often neither warranted nor justified. Sometimes fate just ruins our day. Shit happens, as they say. No one is at fault, so there is no injustice to be rectified. Your bus to work blows a tyre, making you late for an important meeting. Of course, it's annoying; but it is not a moral iniquity, so it does not merit anger. In such instances, we just need to make peace with the fact that the dice were loaded against us that day.

So, if anger begins to bubble up sulphurously, we need to behave like the *Watchful Citizen* who spies a shady figure acting suspiciously on the street. Something may be amiss, some crime might be perpetrated in the near future, but further attention is needed. We should not just sprint outside aggressively to confront the stranger, lashing out in unthinking violence. Instead, we need to monitor the situation carefully. Maybe the stranger is simply waiting for a friend. As soon as that friend arrives, our anger will dissipate, and we can thank our lucky stars that we did not react belligerently before the full facts were known. On the other hand, what if the stranger's suspicious behaviour continues and he disappears into the shadows of a neighbour's garden? In this case, we need to call upon the *Sharp-eyed Detective* to investigate further.

The Sharp-eyed Detective

So, we have decided that we have just cause to be angry. God knows there is much to be angry about. For instance, in Western societies, people of African heritage have long suffered collective injustice and discrimination. The origins of their oppression can be found in the barbarism of slavery, which has blighted humankind since the dawn of recorded history, a perennial example of 'man's inhumanity to man', in the words of Robert Burns. But these iniquities are not simply a poisonous chapter of history, confined to the shameful annals of the past. They persist to this day, as exemplified by the fact that a mass movement has recently formed in the United States to insist that 'black lives matter' after the shooting of numerous black youths by white police officers.

In reflecting on the injustices faced by people of African heritage, and indeed by all people who suffer mistreatment, most of us will feel a stirring of anger. As such, we can clearly see the central proposition of this chapter: anger may be a *moral* emotion. More specifically, Paul Rozin and his colleagues have proposed an influential theory in which anger is presented as a universal human response to violations of *freedom*.[5] This builds upon the work of Richard Shweder, who argued that human life is characterised by three moral spheres, related to the three fundamental ways in which we exist as people.[6] First, we are all autonomous, unique individuals, not simply bricks in a wall or cogs in a machine. This means we all have rights as individual people. Secondly, though, we also exist as parts of a collective. We are not beholden only to ourselves, but are players in the team game of society. This means we have responsibilities towards the group. Finally, we also have a foothold in a kind of sacred dimension. Shweder initially referred to this as the 'sphere of divinity', implying that people share in the divinity of God. But this was later reframed – in language that was more acceptable to secularists – as 'purity/sanctity', meaning an awareness of the preciousness of life itself. Rozin and colleagues then argued that a different moral emotion arises in response to the violation of each of these moral spheres: we feel *anger* if our rights as autonomous individuals are abrogated; we feel *contempt* if someone undermines the solidarity of the group; and we feel *disgust* if the sanctity of life is degraded.

Hence, slavery – the archetypal deprivation of freedom – evokes anger in anyone with a shred of humanity. And yet systemic oppression continues to tarnish Western societies and indeed most other countries around the world. Despite some notable victories – not least by the civil rights movement – people of African heritage still suffer collective injustice. For instance, the freedoms and opportunities of African Americans are still being infringed and compromised even after the election of the first black president of the United States.

The *Watchful Citizen* knows that this is wrong, and feels justifiable anger, but they need help to address it. This is where the *Sharp-eyed Detective* enters the scene, harnessing that anger and carefully gathering the evidence that will clarify the extent of the problem. Indeed, this is what the Black Lives Matter movement is doing right now by clearly and persuasively highlighting the ongoing systemic mistreatment of African Americans. We also see this 'evidence gathering' in the harnessing of technology, such as using smartphones to film authority figures beating civilians, and then disseminating the videos on social media. Similarly, if more traditionally, statistics can shock people into demanding corrective action. For instance, one in every fifteen African-American men is currently in prison, whereas the figure for white men is less than 1 per cent.[7] Meanwhile, the median household income for African Americans is $35,398, against $60,256 for the white population.[8] Then there are personal testimonies, which often have even more of an impact. For instance, I was very moved by Dominique Matti's heartfelt polemic, entitled 'Why I'm Absolutely an Angry Black Woman'. She lays bare the manifold reasons why a woman of colour has a right to feel angry – from the crushing of childhood fantasies (Matti was told that she couldn't be a princess, because 'princesses aren't black'), to witnessing the unfair treatment of loved ones (a school resource officer Maced her brother after he insisted, correctly, that he had not been banned from a football game. The resource officer had mistaken him for another boy). Through her testimony, we can truly appreciate anger as a moral emotion – a just and *necessary* reaction to harm and prejudice.

So, in the guise of the *Sharp-eyed Detective*, our anger helps us enquire into the crimes that we've suffered, detail the nature of our grievances and gather the evidence that will help secure justice. Anger may be harnessed in this way not only when campaigning against serious societal issues, such as the oppression of marginalised groups, but when dealing with more routine yet still exasperating experiences, such as a lack of recognition at work. You may feel unfairly passed over for promotion, or resentful that your hard work has not been appreciated. In such instances, rather than letting your anger eat away at you, try to 'build a case' for why you deserve more recognition by gathering evidence in a clear, objective fashion. Then present it soberly and rationally. This ought to minimise the risk of your justifiable anger being dismissed as a childish craving for attention.

Once you have gathered the evidence, you can then move on to identifying and apprehending those who are responsible for the harm you have suffered. For this, you will need to enlist the services of your inner *Discerning Police Officer*.

The Discerning Police Officer

In the guise of the *Watchful Citizen*, our anger has alerted us to a potential crime; and as the *Sharp-eyed Detective*, it has marshalled the evidence. Now, though, we need to identify the people who have caused our suffering. This may seem straightforward at first, but it is often no easy task. For instance, say a stranger walks up to you in the street and punches you. Of course, he's responsible for the assault. But *why* did he do it? What if we learned he had been abused as a child? Would he still be responsible then? Well, yes, but perhaps not entirely. In terms of apportioning responsibility, surely his abusive parents deserve some of the blame, because they ultimately 'caused' his habitual violence through their mistreatment. But what of *their* upbringing? That may well have been even more harsh, resulting in their abusive nature. And so on, ever further into history, the chain of causation goes. The point is, while we may feel justifiably angry at the person who actually hurts us, when harnessing our anger skilfully it is important to be a *Discerning Police Officer*, concerned with developing a deeper understanding of why a misdeed has occurred. This means striving to see the bigger picture to gain a sense of the complex web of reasons that have resulted in a specific 'crime'. We may even find that most of us are victims in some way. So, rather than blaming a lone wolf, we should perhaps view his act of aggression as a pervasive, systemic issue.

Consider the lingering blight of sexism, and the persistent inequity that women the world over continue to face. It is now more than two centuries since Mary Wollstonecraft wrote the original feminist treatise,[9] and more than a hundred years since Emily Davison perished under the hooves of King George V's horse in the name of women's rights, yet systemic gender inequality still pervades every society. As with racism, this injustice is apparent in the sparse numerals of statistics, such as the fact that women in the UK still earn 19 per cent less than men, on average.[10] We can also find it in countless personal testimonies of sexist mistreatment, which no doubt every woman on Earth has suffered at some point. One recent example springs to mind as particularly illustrative, as it is both ridiculous (in the logic of the abusers) and massively troubling: Caroline Criado-Perez received hundreds of threats – some of them actual *death* threats – on social media after daring to suggest that Jane Austen should appear on the back of the new ten-pound banknote.

This deeply unjust state of affairs – in which women are collectively held back, victimised and oppressed – has a name: patriarchy, which literally means 'rule of the father'. It rightly provokes anger – not only among women, but within all people who strive for equality. In order to address it, though, we must ask: whose *fault* is it? Here we must explore the *system* of patriarchy itself. Is it simply the collective manifestation of men's inherent sexism? Or is something deeper, more insidious at work here, a spider's web of inherited traditions and processes that may also damage men themselves? In researching my PhD – which focused on the impact of gender on mental health – I read of an escalating 'crisis of men'. This was vividly highlighted in a barrage of alarming statistics relating to a wide range of subjects – from mental health (men account for three-quarters of all suicides[11]), to crime (men constitute 95 per cent of the UK's prison population[12]). Clearly, whatever patriarchy is, and whatever benefits it may confer upon men – for instance, in terms of personal freedom or earning potential – in other ways many males are suffering because of it.

Acknowledging this fact does not mean absolving men from any blame. Of course, any individual man who mistreats and abuses a woman must be held to account. But it does mean that there are also bigger battles to be fought. We need to turn our attention to changing a system in which men are encouraged and even coerced into adopting roles that are injurious to women (and often to themselves, too). For instance, many women have suffered sexist treatment in the workplace. Indeed, many of my female friends and family members have related troubling stories of sexism within organisations that I had naively assumed would be more enlightened. It makes them – and me – justifiably angry. I care what happens to them, I want them to flourish, so I know that sexism is not just *their* battle, but a struggle that concerns me, too. This goes for all men: we all have women in our lives whom we care about, so we all need to join their campaign for a fairer system.

The key word here is 'system'. Every abusive man who indulges in sexist nonsense should be corrected, reprimanded and educated. But we also need to change the system in order to dismantle the sexism that is structurally embedded throughout society. In academia, for example, this means creating initiatives such as 'Athena SWAN' (the Scientific Women's Academic Network), which aims to encourage and support women's scientific research by breaking down access barriers and pushing for pay equality. No doubt most fields of endeavour have similarly laudable organisations. We should all – men and women – offer them our support and encouragement.

Then, once our inner *Discerning Police Officer* has sensitised us to the complexities of responsibility and blame, we must enlist the help of the *Eloquent Prosecutor* to fight the battle itself.

The Eloquent Prosecutor

In one of my earliest memories, I am sitting on my dad's shoulders, looking out over a tumultuous sea of banners, a kaleidoscope of colour. There is always something carnivalesque about a protest march – an intoxicating whirl of spirit and solidarity. I was fortunate to be blessed with two wonderful, loving parents, who barely raised their voices to me and nurtured me through gentle kindness. At the same time, they always had – and still have – a heartfelt concern about the iniquities of society, so my childhood was suffused with their passion for justice. I remember many a cold morning, huddled among crowds of like-minded souls, marching for a raft of progressive causes – from women's liberation, to nuclear disarmament. We were active participants in a proud tradition of peaceful protest, the power of which has reverberated around the world. Such dissent has proved to be one of the most persuasive tools a citizenry can wield in the service of correcting injustice or changing an invidious system. As a form of precisely channelled anger, it is the very embodiment of the *Eloquent Prosecutor*.

Sometimes protesting demands great courage and determination, especially in highly charged arenas. While the
London protests of my childhood were generally fairly
safe and untroubled affairs, many other people have taken
immense risks to make their voices heard, even to the point
of laying their lives on the line. The two legendary figures
who are most associated with peaceful protest – Martin
Luther King, architect of the US civil rights movement, and
Mahatma Gandhi, whose ethic of non-violence inspired Dr
King – were both assassinated in the service of their cause.
But they and their movements were undoubtedly more powerful because they refused to cede the moral high ground,
irrespective of the grievous provocation and retribution
that were wreaked upon them. Goodness knows, both men
must have been tempted to lash out against their oppres-
sors on numerous occasions. But, *Eloquent Prosecutors* that
they were, they knew this would weaken their case in the
eyes of society and lead to accusations of rabble-rousing.
Moreover, Dr King preached, with unmatched rhetorical
force, that reacting to violence only breeds further violence,
in a destructive downward spiral of hate that lays waste to
everyone. Instead, he urged his supporters to follow Jesus's
revolutionary code and treat their enemies with love and
compassion, even while maintaining the righteous anger
that fuelled their struggle.

The eloquent pursuit of justice can take many forms. One
of the most powerful mechanisms of redress that has emerged
over the last few centuries is the trade union movement,
which advocates and organises for better working conditions. As with protest marches, trade unionism harnesses
the strength of the collective voice, utilising the energy and

sense of security that can arise from solidarity in a common cause. But it has often been dangerous terrain for those involved, who have suffered the backlash of vested interests and repression from the establishment. For instance, in the UK, where the trade union movement arose in response to the dehumanising conditions of the Industrial Revolution, the government criminalised unionism in 1799, fearful of a civil uprising. Although these laws were repealed twenty-five years later, political power remained in the hands of a wealthy aristocracy, so the unions continued to face significant and well-organised opposition for many more years. For example, in 1834, six agricultural workers from a village in Dorset – the so-called Tolpuddle Martyrs – were arrested for union activity and deported to Australia. And even harsher repression continues to this day. In the Philippines in 2015, Florencio Romano became the eighteenth union leader in that country to be assassinated for his activities in the course of just five years.[13]

Clearly, then, speaking truth to power can sometimes be extremely dangerous. But it can also be ennobling, embodying a spirit of courage and ethical purpose. Personally, my parents have inspired me greatly. For instance, during his years of dedicated work as a college lecturer, my dad must have devoted thousands of hours to his parallel responsibilities as a union representative. It fell to him to defend any employees who found themselves out of favour with the powers that be. Some of these were scapegoats, blamed for failings outside of their control, while others faced trumped-up charges because of personal differences with authority figures. My dad was often angry at the unfairness of it all, and felt compelled to fight on the victims' behalf. This was not glamorous or well-remunerated work, but there was real worth and dignity in it. He spoke out for those who lacked a voice and power, and garnered great respect as a result. Then, ultimately, he would appeal to a jury – usually in the form of a tribunal – to reach the right decision.

The Merciful Juror

There is a powerful scene in Steven Spielberg's masterpiece, *Schindler's List*, in which Itzhak Stern, Oskar Schindler's accountant and moral compass, is in conversation with Amon Goeth, the sadistic camp commandant. In that hell on Earth, Goeth wields absolute power. And with it, he indulges his vilest whims, up to and including the summary execution of children. Attempting to evoke a sliver of humanity within this monster, Stern relates the parable of a king who exerts total and wrathful authority over his subjects, all of whom live in mortal fear of him. One day, a subject is brought trembling before the ruler. Although guilty of committing only a minor infraction, the poor man fully expects to be sentenced to death. And yet . . . the king forgives him and sets him free. Stern looks Goeth in his cold, unfeeling eyes, and whispers, 'Now *that* is power.' The dual message – which is lost on the commandant, who is beyond redemption – is that showing mercy is not weakness, and control does not have to be maintained through aggression and force. On the contrary, mercy may be the ultimate demonstration of power and the best means of exerting authority.

I would not dare to tell anyone how they must respond to mistreatment. I've said before that I want to avoid 'shoulds' in this book. So, if someone has hurt you deeply, I have no right to say that you should forgive them; that, as a *juror* of their crime, you must be merciful. Only you will know the harm they have caused, and what punishment is just. Given that we can feel helpless in so many areas of life, though, battered around by huge forces that are beyond our control – from the merciless tides of economic trends, to the life-altering policies that are formulated in the government's ivory towers – one area in which we *can* still exercise control is in how we respond to maltreatment. Sometimes, this is all we have, as Albert Camus pointed out in *The Rebel*.[14] Even if a slave is hobbled and chained, unable to free himself from the cruel whips of his masters, they will never have dominion over his mind. Try as they might to dehumanise him, he can still say, 'No, I am a man.' So, when anger compels us to judge the guilt of those who have wounded us, we can draw some strength from knowing that we retain at least some degree of power and control, because we may choose to respond either with or without mercy. And if we *do* show mercy, this may be important not only for those we judge but for ourselves, as victims. I spoke earlier of the danger of allowing anger to turn into hatred, which can often be even more destructive to the hater than it is to the object of their hatred. Remaining compassionate can thus be one of the most effective ways of preventing righteous anger from becoming poisonous vitriol. As such, it is to *our* advantage to express anger in a merciful, compassionate way.

Recently, I read the heartbreaking story of a woman who we'll call Susan (not her real name). The day before Mother's Day, her precious daughter Jill returned from university and went out with a friend. Later that evening, Jill called to say she would be back the next morning, and told her mother that she loved her. It was the last time that Susan would hear her daughter's voice. A couple of hours later, a drunk-driver hit Jill and her friend's car and killed them instantly. Susan was forced to spend Mother's Day identifying her daughter's body. Words cannot begin to articulate the unfathomable grief and shock that she must have felt, but also her fury at the man who had taken her daughter's life through his senseless irresponsibility. Her anger escalated at the subsequent trial, when the driver, seemingly cold and wholly unrepentant, pleaded not guilty. Susan hoped he would receive the maximum sentence, which she felt would be deserved retribution not only for his crime but for his callous refusal to take responsibility for his actions. She judged his guilt to be absolute, as surely anyone else in her position would.

Before the judge passed sentence, however, Susan received a letter from the driver. In contrast to his demeanour in court, it revealed a man who was consumed by remorse. Indeed, he wrote that he had wanted to apologise during the trial, but his lawyer had instructed him to say nothing. He was not a heartless sociopath, he said, but had made a terrible mistake that would haunt him all his life. The thought of forgiveness had previously entered Susan's mind, but she had banished it while the driver had seemed unrepentant. Now, though, with his heartfelt contrition in mind, at the sentencing she ended her statement to the court by saying, 'I forgive you.' This was a truly heroic and magnanimous act of generosity that offered a thread of salvation to a broken young man. But it was also a vital step on Susan's own road to recovery. She did not want to live out the rest of her days 'consumed by bitterness', so she found some peace in being a *Merciful Juror*. She still felt the driver deserved punishment, but, while hating the sin, she was able to find compassion for the sinner and see him as just another flawed human being. After all, everybody sins, even if the consequences are not always as tragic as they were in this case. We are all wrought from the same 'crooked timber of humanity', in Isaiah Berlin's haunting phrase.

Compassion and forgiveness are important themes throughout this book. In Susan's case, granting mercy helped her live again. That said, I don't know if I would be strong enough to do likewise, and I pray that I am never tested in a similar way. In your own trials, only you will know if forgiveness feels right and will be helpful to you. So, if granting mercy as a *Merciful Juror*, remember most importantly to also bestow it on *yourself*. This can be difficult, as our harshest judgements are frequently reserved for ourselves. Hence, psychologists like Kristen Neff advocate exercises that are proving effective at boosting self-compassion.[15] For instance, one of the most powerful techniques to generate compassion – for oneself and others – is loving-kindness meditation.[16] This has its roots in Buddhism, but you certainly don't need to be a Buddhist – or even remotely spiritual – to derive great benefit from it. It is simply a good place to start for anyone who is looking to develop compassion. Whatever you choose to do, though, and however you decide to assess the guilt of your aggressors, try to remain compassionate towards yourself. Remember that you are doing your best in awful circumstances that no one should ever have to face.

Once guilt has been established, we need to figure out the most appropriate means and degree of redress. For this, we need to be a *Wise Judge*.

The Wise Judge

It is early morning on 24 April 2013, seemingly just another Wednesday in Dhaka, Bangladesh. But an unusual scene is reportedly unfolding outside the Rana Plaza factory.[17] The eight-storey concrete structure houses over 3500 workers, 80 per cent of them young women between the ages of eighteen and twenty, most of whom work up to a hundred hours a week for as little as twelve cents an hour. Their task is to make clothes that Western multinationals will sell at 'bargain' prices to their affluent European and American consumers. Today, though, large cracks have begun to appear in the outer walls of the building. The workers, fearing for their safety, refuse to enter. However, the workers of one business allege that they were forced to enter due to threats to withhold their food and pay for a month. At 8 a.m., the workers reluctantly walk inside and set to work. Forty-five minutes later, the lights go out, and the factory's emergency generators kick in. Almost immediately, the tower begins to sway. Then there is a deafening explosion. The tower collapses. A week later, 1137 workers, all of whom had spent most of their young lives toiling for pennies, are confirmed dead.

A swathe of studies confirms the obvious: most people are enraged by this kind of callous indifference to occupational welfare, when even basic safety is disregarded in the unrelenting pursuit of profit. For instance, Silvia Grappi and colleagues presented volunteers with hypothetical examples of corporate irresponsibility and showed that anger escalates in relation to the perceived degree of ethical violation.[18] Of course, even the most *Merciful Jurors* will pronounce such buccaneering companies guilty. But to harness our anger skilfully, for it to have any impact, we must go beyond issuing that simple verdict. We need to become a *Wise Judge* and determine the most appropriate and effective form of 'punishment'. The word 'wise' is key here. Unthoughtful vengeance will be counterproductive. So we must try to impose a penalty that will have the best chance of changing the situation and/or correcting the behaviour that we found so grievous.

In the case of corporate misdeeds, we may feel weary disgust against seemingly untouchable multinationals, lamenting, 'How can they do that? How can they mistreat their workers so badly?', yet assuming that we can do nothing to punish them. But that is not true. First, we need to accept that 'we' are 'they'. An unethical corporation is not a wild animal, wreaking havoc in isolation. Rather, it lies at the centre of a vast, toxic spider's web, and *we* are the strands of that web. Profitable multinationals are created and sustained by *our* actions, and by the actions of millions of other consumers. Our desire for ever-cheaper clothing, regardless of ethical provenance, plays a pivotal role in creating the conditions for atrocities like Rana Plaza, and for modern-day wage slavery more generally.

This is a chastening realisation, but it is also empowering. Because, if we are partly responsible for workers' exploitation, we can do something about it. We have numerous retributive tools at our disposal to effect corporate change – from demonstrations and boycotts, to word-of-mouth and social media campaigns. Never forget that most corporations care about their profit margins above all else. While this is ethically dispiriting, it is pragmatically useful. For, if we reward ethical companies with our custom, and punish unethical ones by refusing to buy their products, we can and will make a difference. A few days before I started writing this chapter, for instance, a British supermarket suddenly decided to remove all of the charity collection points from its stores. This angered many people, and a boycott campaign soon gathered momentum. As a result, the supermarket – acutely conscious of preserving its profits and reputation – rapidly relented and reinstalled the collection points. It was a good example of how swiftly and successfully consumer pressure can deliver positive ethical results.

We can also strive to be a *Wise Judge* with regard to more personal crimes. Consider the awful problem of domestic abuse, from which a third of women around the world have suffered.[19] In such situations, the overriding, urgent priority is to halt the abuse, either by compelling the abuser to stop or by facilitating the victim's escape. Here, the *Judge*'s task is to determine how best to achieve one of these two outcomes. James McNulty and Peter Fincham have conducted important work in this field.[20] Their research questions the extent to which emotions that we normally view as 'positive' – such as forgiveness – should be regarded as such in abusive situations. Once people have escaped from an abusive relationship, they may indeed benefit from cultivating some level of forgiveness towards their former abuser.[21] But displaying such forgiveness while still within such a relationship can be problematic, as it might inadvertently perpetuate the situation. Needless to say, it is not McNulty and Fincham's intention to place any blame on the victims. Rather, they are trying to help the injured parties hold their aggressors to account.

Ultimately, of course, we need to establish the most appropriate correction and punishment for the guilty party, and once again this demands careful consideration. With that, we come to the final role of anger: the *Rehabilitative Prison Governor.*

The Rehabilitative Prison Governor

We have seen that anger can be a moral emotion, a visceral sign that all is not right in the world. Moreover, if it is harnessed skilfully, it can play an important role in redressing these wrongs. And that harnessing must indeed be skilful, because the alternative is that anger corrodes into hate, which will worsen the situation for everyone, not least ourselves. If used deftly, though, anger can serve a range of vital functions that together can help to make the world a better place. And the final role in this process is played by the *Rehabilitative Prison Governor* – the figure who enforces the 'punishment'.

The notion of rehabilitation is crucial here. When we punish someone in anger, there will often be an entirely understandable desire for retribution: for the guilty party to suffer, just as we have suffered. The concept of an eye for an eye is as old as humankind, and it does indeed encompass some essential sense of justice and fairness. But pursuing this type of punitive equivalence is a dangerous road to take. People who have chosen an alternative path suggest that it may be better to aim for the high road and seek our aggressors' rehabilitation, even when the thought pains us. The essential point here is that following this higher path is not ultimately about them, and their recovery, but about you, and your rehabilitation. Obviously, rehabilitation is far better than punitive punishment from the criminal's perspective: the former may be his pathway back to civilisation, while the latter will likely lead him further into the darkness. But we might be tempted to think, 'So what? He had it coming. Once he's locked up, why do I care what becomes of him?' For truly heinous crimes, this may be the only possible response, and the only way to move on with our lives. Either way though, *we*, the victims, certainly need to experience rehabilitation; and this can often be aided if those who have hurt us experience its benefits, too.

Research has found that a tragedy or a crime is much harder to process, to bear and to recover from if it is *senseless* – if it was committed for no reason or purpose. Consequently, victims of trauma who are able to find some kind of meaning in what has happened to them tend to experience more effective recoveries.[22] For some people, this sense of meaning can be found by perceiving a spiritual dimension to their suffering, such as viewing it as part of 'God's plan', or thinking that a loved one has 'gone to a better place'. For others, the meaning might be found through leaving some kind of legacy, as in the brave and noble actions of people who fight for an inquest after a tragic bereavement. In such cases, the avowed intention is usually to save future people from suffering a similar fate. Of course, the campaigner knows that this will not bring back their loved one, but at least it will mean that their death was not entirely in vain, and some good may come of it.

Susan took just such a selfless and heroic path. Having offered the man who killed her daughter some forgiveness, her path of rehabilitation – both for the drunk-driver and for herself – did not stop there. She started giving anti-drink-driving talks to young people, in the hope of preventing future tragedies. Moreover, she invited the driver to join her at these events. Whatever rehabilitative role this may have played in his life – and it surely did – the sight of him standing alongside her must have been immeasurably powerful for the audience, creating a powerful message that no doubt did save lives, just as Susan hoped it would.

So, whatever hurt has been visited upon you, whatever anger you feel towards those who have caused you suffering, there may be some salvation in delivering justice in a way that is rehabilitative, above all for yourself. This is the final piece of the process of using anger to change our world for the better.

Sometimes, though, *we* may be the one who is in the wrong, hurting others and meriting *their* anger. In such cases, we have to wrestle with guilt, as the next chapter explores.

CHAPTER FOUR

Guilt

Of all the heart-rending scenes in theatre, few are as powerful as the eerie descent of Lady Macbeth into madness. Spellbound, we see her furiously trying to wash imagined blood off her hands in a vain attempt to erase and atone for her collusion in the murder of King Duncan, plaintively crying out: 'Will these hands ne'er be clean.' Modern research confirms that Shakespeare was a shrewd psychologist. Chen-Bo Zhong and Katie Liljenquist found that a sense of guilt can indeed make people want to cleanse themselves, as if their misdeeds have led them to feel physically contaminated, and in need of purification.[1] The researchers asked one group of volunteers to dwell on a past misdeed (the 'immoral group'), and another to recall a good deed (the 'moral group'). Everyone was then offered a gift for taking part in the experiment – either a pencil or an antiseptic wipe. Nearly all of those in the moral group opted for the pencil, while those in the immoral group were much more likely to choose the wipe – perhaps in the hope of washing away their sins. Similarly, in a second part of the study,[2] another set of participants were asked to reflect on a past transgression. Later, some of them were given an antiseptic wipe to clean their hands, while the others received nothing. All of the participants were then asked if they would be willing to help out with a future research project. Those who had cleansed themselves – both physically and thus also metaphorically – were less likely to volunteer than the unwashed group, who presumably still felt tainted by their misdeeds.

Aside from the fascinating intertwining of guilt and cleanliness, the lesson of these studies is that guilt can help us become better people. We can think of it as the counterpart to anger. Both can be moral emotions; the only difference is the target. Whereas anger is directed at others, when we feel guilty we focus the condemnation on ourselves. As the previous chapter explained, anger may be a moral response to an unjust situation, and it can be a powerful agent in correcting iniquities. Similarly, if someone accepts responsibility for causing, upholding or otherwise contributing to a misdeed, the results can be highly beneficial. And most of us are guilty of something, in some way, at some time. None of us is perfect, but we can all strive to be good, or at least better than we are. This, then, is the value of guilt: as with anger, it can form part of our moral compass. It is our intuitive sense of the ways in which we have erred, and is thus a vital source of information about the quality of our past actions. Unfortunately, we may sometimes feel excessive guilt, or guilt that is not warranted at all. But *appropriate* guilt, acknowledged through compassionate and considered self-reflection, can be a positive spur, prompting us towards redress, towards goodness.

Disentangling Guilt, Shame and Humiliation

As we become better acquainted with guilt, we may also get to know its two rough-hewn associates – shame and humiliation. Lost in the fog of self-preoccupation, sometimes we don't notice our misdeeds. This is not necessarily due to insensitivity. Rather, we may be so weighed down by our own burdens that we don't realise we've veered clumsily into the path of a fellow traveller. In those situations, we may need a short, sharp nudge from others to appreciate the error of our ways.

Of course, shame and humiliation are both highly unpleasant emotions. As such, we need to be wary of colluding in the kind of mob mentality that delights in the downfall of others, as Jon Ronson has charted so disturbingly.[3] This vicious crowd-based victimisation has unfortunately become even more prevalent with the rise of social media, given the ease with which people are now able to whip up a 'Twitter storm' and spark a frenzy of condemnation for a person who may have acted or spoken insensitively. This is not to say that all public criticism should be outlawed – sometimes it is entirely justified. But mob shamings can veer dangerously into self-righteousness and aggression, seeking to bring down a person for what may have been no more than an ill-judged tweet. You will find no generosity of spirit in these electronic witch-hunts. None of the victims ever receives the benefit of the doubt. Their attackers rarely seek to understand their intentions or try to contextualise their behaviour. And they display precious little compassion for the suddenly humiliated victim.

That said, though, if we find ourselves suffering shame or humiliation, we may encounter some benefits amid the unpleasantness, diamonds in the mud. If, on reflection, we realise that our shame and humiliation are merited, such experiences can teach us some valuable lessons. Consider the fact that, etymologically, humiliation is closely related to humility – both words stem from the Latin term for 'lowly' – which has long been celebrated as a virtue. So, what if we were able to transform our humiliating experiences into a sense of humility, a recognition that we are fallible? Shame and humiliation – *as long as they are warranted and proportionate* – can be the means through which the world tells us that we have erred, that we have good reason to feel guilty. In turn, guilt can serve as a moral emotion, a motivating force that will help us steer our lives towards more prosperous futures. The same could be said for regret, which is essentially a melancholic form of guilt, a lamentation of past actions. Many people say, 'No regrets,' but none of us is infallible, so we all surely have *some* cause for regret. This can be a good thing . . . if we learn to use it wisely.

You may be weighed down by guilt, perhaps after hurting a loved one. You are not alone – all but the most sainted of us carry these kinds of burdens deep inside. Crucially, though, rather than wishing away your guilt, you can turn it into a powerful learning experience. Any attempt to understand it indicates a desire to change and become a better person. Indeed, it is often only when we reflect deeply on our errors that we find the motivation to develop and grow. So, if we have done wrong, our duty – and our salvation – lies in examining those misdeeds and reflecting upon the hurt we have caused. Importantly, such introspection must not degenerate into drowning in self-hatred. Rather, we need to consider our past actions in a self-compassionate spirit, and then channel the resulting guilt in fruitful ways, using it to jolt ourselves into better patterns of behaviour. This process helps us to treat others with greater kindness, consideration and respect, which in turn has a beneficial effect on our own lives. For you don't have to embrace the concept of karma to realise that the better you treat people, the better they tend to treat you in return.

In this chapter, then, we explore how to harness guilt skilfully and use it to shape our lives for the better. First, though, we need to understand that a variety of different motivations drive our behaviour, so, in consequence, there are several types of guilt, as the next section explores.

The Spectrum of Motivation

In a small town, a woman is in bed with a high fever. Her husband, Hans, is understandably frantic with concern and dashes to the doctor, begging for help. The doctor tells him that Rolf, the town's chemist, has a drug in stock that will cure his wife's illness. Hans races over to the pharmacy and asks for the drug. Rolf fetches the bottle and tells Hans that the cost is £2000. This extortionate sum is far beyond Hans's meagre means, so, in tears, he explains the gravity of the situation and begs Rolf to lower the price. But the chemist is a ruthless businessman who has never allowed sentimentality to erode his profit margins. Hans tries to negotiate. He suggests paying £200 now (all the money he has) and settling up the remainder over the next year. Rolf still refuses to budge, so Hans dashes out of the shop and knocks on every door, asking each of his neighbours for a loan. His friends are generous, but Hans manages to collect only £1000. The situation seems hopeless, so, that night, Hans does something he has never done before: he breaks the law. He climbs through the window of the pharmacy and steals the drug. His beloved wife is brought back from the brink of death and makes a full recovery.

All of us would be tempted to do the same if we found ourselves in this kind of awful situation; and most of us would probably behave precisely as Hans did and steal the drug. But the crucial question is: was he *right* to do so? And if your answer is 'Yes, of course,' on what *basis* was he right? This was what Lawrence Kohlberg aimed to discover when he devised the scenario described above.[4] His research focused on moral reasoning: essentially, why we do what we do, and how we justify our actions to ourselves. He posed Hans's dilemma to thousands of people, asking them if they thought he was right to steal the drug; and if so, why? Over the course of this lengthy research project, six main answers emerged – half a dozen overarching ways in which people attempted to explain and account for Hans's behaviour. Hence, Kohlberg suggested that human beings are driven by six distinct motivations – different reasons why they might choose and justify a particular action in their own lives. This *spectrum of motivation* can help us understand our own behaviour. Most of us have probably been driven by many – if not all – of the six motivations at one time or another. And, if we misbehave, we experience distinct types of guilt, depending on the motivation that drove our actions. Moreover, these forms of guilt are not all equal: some are 'better' than others. As such, even if we never manage to become entirely guilt free, at least we can strive to develop more *positive* forms of guilt, and so become better versions of ourselves.

The first two reasons that people gave to explain and justify Hans's behaviour were based on what the *personal* outcome would be for him. Kohlberg called these 'pre-conventional' motivations: they are not guided by 'convention' (laws or social norms) but by fear of punishment and expectation of reward. In the first – which Kohlberg labelled 'obedience and punishment' – we are motivated to act or not on the basis of whether we believe we will be punished as a result. Personifying this metaphorically, we could call this motivation our inner *Obedient Servant*. Anyone considering Hans's plight from this perspective would probably argue that he *should not* steal the drug, because he might be caught and arrested. You will almost certainly have followed this line of reasoning yourself – and will have experienced the related form of guilt – if you've ever done something that you know is wrong in order to avoid unwelcome consequences. Engaging in shady or unethical activity at work because of pressure from a boss would be a prime example. The second type of pre-conventional motivation shifts the focus from punishment to reward: we act on the basis of what we want or need, regardless of whether it is right to do so. In such instances we are guided by our inner *Jewel Thief*. From this perspective, it could be argued that Hans *should* steal the drug, simply because he wants it. If you've ever done something wrong out of greedy self-interest – such as stealing something or lying to advance your career – you will be familiar with this form of reasoning, and the specific brand of guilt that arises from it.

Kohlberg described the next pair of motivations as 'conventional', since they are based on *society*'s laws and norms, rather than personal fears and aspirations. He labelled the first of these the 'good boy/girl' attitude. Here, people consider what will meet with society's approval and act accordingly. In other words, they are guided by their inner *People Pleaser*. Looking at Hans's dilemma from this perspective, one could argue that he *should* steal the drug, since he will incur the wrath of his family and friends if he does not do everything in his power to save his wife. You will be familiar with this reasoning, and the concomitant guilt, if you've ever done something that you know to be wrong simply to fit in with a group or win its approval. The second conventional motivation is 'authority and social order'. Here, the rule of law dictates our behaviour and allows us to rationalise it. This encompasses everything from the legislation that governs society, to the prescriptions of religious traditions. In this chapter, I have termed the inner personification of this perspective the *Conscientious Rule Keeper*. A person guided by this might sympathise with Hans's predicament, but would still argue that he *should not* take the law into his own hands. If you've ever stuck rigidly to a rule – even if you were tempted to break it – you have been guided by this line of reasoning. For instance, picture a policeman who pulls over a speeding car to learn that the driver is a panicking mother who is rushing her child to hospital, but then issues the ticket anyway because his primary duty is to uphold the law.

Finally, Kohlberg identified two forms of motivation that he described as 'post-conventional'. In such circumstances, we reach the conclusion that society's conventional laws are flawed, so we adopt what is – to our mind at least – a 'higher' perspective. The first such motivation is known as the 'social contract'. Here, we recognise that laws are human creations that are contingent upon culture, often flawed and, most importantly, amenable to improvement if they are deficient. Thus, we can and should work to enhance them on the basis of mutual agreement. I call this motivation our inner *Social Reformer*. From this perspective, you may feel it's wrong for the law to prioritise profit-making over care for the needy, and so argue that Hans *should* steal the drug (and indeed that the law should be changed). If you've ever worked to improve a set of rules that you felt were deficient, then you'll be familiar with the social contract. Similarly, when guided by the final motivation – 'universal principles' – we feel that moral judgements should be based on ideals that transcend societal consensus. One aspect of this perspective is usually that human life is sacred, so Hans *should* steal the drug, regardless of what anyone else might think of his behaviour. I call the inner personification of this motivation the *Principled Idealist*. If you've ever taken a stand about something – especially if you had to make your case alone – then you have been influenced by this line of reasoning.

As we shall see, all six of the motivations and justifications identified by Kohlberg can help us make sense of our actions. Moreover, we can use these reflections to try to develop and grow as people. Kohlberg suggested that the world would be a better place if more people were guided by the later motivations, particularly the post-conventional ones. He regarded the six motivations like the rungs of a ladder, enabling us to climb to ever higher levels of development, and consequently to attain more fulfilling states of wellbeing. Therefore, we will explore how guilt may be used to help us move up from the lower-level motivations (the *Obedient Servant* and the *Jewel Thief*) and towards the pinnacle of the *Principled Idealist*. For instance, you may feel guilty about a time when your inner *Jewel Thief* drove you to behave selfishly. By dwelling on this regret, you may be empowered to follow more elevated motives in future, such as concern for others. This kind of psychological development is important because it's the key to a flourishing, ethically rich life. As some of the world's most renowned psychologists – from Abraham Maslow[5] to Carl Jung[6] – have shown, the more we try to become better people, the happier and more fulfilled we tend to be. With that in mind, let's explore each of the motivations in turn.

The Obedient Servant

Do you think you could kill someone? Perhaps you might consider it in an extreme situation, say in a desperate act of self-defence. But otherwise, certainly not? Shockingly, an infamous experiment suggests you might be less immune to the possibility than you would suspect. In 1961, Stanley Milgram invited a group of New Haven citizens into his lab to take part in an 'experiment on learning'.[7] He assigned the participants into one of two groups: teachers or learners. Each of the teachers was then placed alone in a room, in front of a machine with some ominous-looking switches. Next they were told that one of students was in another room and would be tested on a series of questions. If the student answered incorrectly, the teacher was told to flick the first switch. This was where things got shocking, literally, because the switch supposedly administered a 15-volt electric shock to the student, as a label on the machine indicated. Should the student make a subsequent error, the teacher was obliged to flick the second switch. This time, the student would receive 30 volts. And so on, at 15-volt increments, all the way up to 450 volts. Flicking this final switch – as the label on the machine warned – would result in 'certain death'. In reality, of course, it was an elaborate set-up: the students were all actors and suffered no electric shocks. But the experiment was very convincing. At first, the students would simply scream for mercy. At 300 volts, they would bang frantically on the interconnecting wall, begging the teacher to stop. Thereafter, they stopped responding altogether, seemingly incapacitated by pain or already dead. Understandably, the teachers – some of whom became highly distressed – protested to the researcher and pleaded with him to stop the trial. In response, the researcher merely shouted, 'You must go on!'

Before commencing the project, Milgram asked forty eminent psychiatrists to predict how far the teachers would go. The consensus was that fewer than 4 per cent would flick any of the switches above 300 volts, and that just 0.1 per cent – essentially a rogue psychopath who had somehow infiltrated the experiment – would go all the way. Consequently, the results shocked the world: two-thirds of the teachers went all the way to the maximum 450 volts. In other words, they were prepared to kill a complete stranger for failing at a silly word game simply because someone in a white coat told them to.

While these findings would be deeply worrying in any context, they were particularly troubling given the grim events that were unfolding halfway around the world at the time. The trial of Adolf Eichmann, the Nazi officer who was responsible for organising mass deportations of Europe's Jews to the extermination camps, had begun in Jerusalem three months earlier and was still ongoing when Milgram conducted his experiment. Before the war, Eichmann had led an unremarkable existence, working as a sales clerk, before rising to the upper echelons of the Nazi hierarchy. Indeed, at his trial, he seemed to be a very ordinary – even dull – man, more like a diligent book-keeper than a homicidal tyrant. Yet he was pivotal in orchestrating the vilest and most extensive act of genocide the world has ever seen. Covering the trial, Hannah Arendt famously coined the phrase 'the banality of evil' to describe this kind of ghoulish disjunction.[8] As ever more details of Eichmann's crimes continued to emerge, Milgram's study took on especially sinister overtones.

In the traumatic aftermath of the Second World War, among the many questions a shell-shocked world asked itself, one of the most urgent was: were the Nazis *uniquely* evil? If they were, although the world could never forget or forgive the barbarities of the Holocaust, at least we could persuade ourselves that it was a catastrophic aberration that would never be repeated. But what if the Nazis were simply ordinary human beings – regular, 'banal' people – who somehow agreed to commit unspeakable acts of violence? If that were the case, similar deadly potential could be lying dormant in all of us, and might be similarly awoken in extraordinary – or even quite mundane – circumstances. On the stand in Jerusalem, Eichmann seemed to indicate that the latter scenario was more likely. Apparently untroubled by guilt, he denied all responsibility for his actions with the infamous claim that he was merely following orders. It was just such a nihilistic claim that Milgram wished to explore. Could he convince an average American citizen to kill someone simply by ordering them to flick a switch? It seemed that he could, at least two-thirds of the time. His experiment held up a bleak mirror to humanity, and the world recoiled.

According to Kohlberg's framework, Milgram's participants were driven by an overriding concern for 'obedience and punishment'. In other words, they behaved like *Obedient Servants*. They acted as they did simply because somebody in authority told them to, and they feared the repercussions of not obeying the authority figure's orders. Most of them must have known that what they were doing was wrong – hence their vociferous but in most cases ultimately hollow protestations. Indeed, we might assume that the 'teachers' were familiar with the other inner figures that appear in this chapter, and that these figures were all protesting loudly inside their minds. For instance, the *Conscientious Rule Keeper* may well have raised objections on the basis that they were breaking the law by electrocuting the students, while the *Principled Idealist* would have put a strong case for the sanctity of human life. And yet, urged on by the researcher, most of the teachers continued to behave as *Obedient Servants*. Their fear of punishment made them act in an utterly barbaric way.

We have probably all done things that we later regretted due to this kind of obedience. Maybe your boss pressured you into doing something you felt was unethical, but you went ahead and did it because you were worried about being disciplined or even fired for disobeying a direct order. For instance, when I worked for a catering company, I greatly resented their policy of throwing away unused food, rather than giving it to local charities. Yet I did as I was told and chucked it in the bin, afraid of being remanded, and I've subsequently felt guilty about my acquiescence.

If you are familiar with this kind of guilt, I'd like to offer two pieces of advice. First, try to have some compassion for yourself, as you did not ask to be put in that predicament. It's very difficult to say 'no' to people in power, especially if they can wield significant punishments. Indeed, in some ways, your guilt may be mitigated – depending on the severity of the crime – by the extent to which you were coerced by authority figures (who ought to shoulder some of the blame). As we saw in the previous chapter, it is vital to maintain a sense of self-compassion, and not to succumb to self-recrimination that we do not deserve. That said, my second piece of advice is that if, on reflection, your guilt seems appropriate, try to learn from it and avoid making similar mistakes in the future. Let's return to Milgram's experiment for a moment. While the headline results were extremely disturbing, a lesser-known aspect of the study was rather more reassuring. One might presume that the whole exercise was deeply humiliating for the 'teachers', leaving a painful legacy of guilt over how easily they had been coerced into wrongdoing. And the participants did indeed report that it was a hugely troubling experience. Nevertheless, 84 per cent of them also said that they were either 'very glad' or 'glad' to have taken part, with only 1 per cent regretting their participation.

Although the experience was undoubtedly mortifying, they were grateful for the lessons they learned about themselves: not only about their all-too-human failings, but about the importance of staying true to their moral beliefs, and not allowing themselves to be compromised or coerced by authority. Indeed, this is where such people differ fundamentally from monsters like the unrepentant Eichmann: they feel the redemptive moral presence of *guilt*. Such guilt may be life-changing. For instance, one of the participants wrote to Milgram years after the experiment, at the height of the Vietnam War, to thank him. He explained that his guilt over his actions that day had emboldened him to follow his principles ever since. He was now a conscientious objector, taking a bold stand of defiance for which he was prepared to go to jail.

So, reflective guilt over those occasions when our *Obedient Servant* has driven our actions can empower us to resist such behaviour in the future. And a similar process can occur with our inner *Jewel Thief.*

The Jewel Thief

Imagine you are a brazen jewel thief, living royally off your illicit activities. One day, though, your luck runs out. The lord of a stately manor spots you and your partner in crime in the gardens, then notices that his priceless pocket watch is missing from the dresser. He calls the police, who promptly haul you and your fellow outlaw to the local station. Both you and your accomplice are clearly guilty of trespass, as the police arrested you on the lord of the manor's land. This crime carries a maximum penalty of one year in prison. But proving that either you or your partner in crime stole the watch – which would incur five years inside – is far trickier as neither of you had the watch on your person when you were arrested. Therefore, the prosecution team will be able to secure a guilty verdict only if you or your co-conspirator betrays the other and blames them for the theft.

During your interrogation, you are presented with four scenarios:

- Option A: You inform on your partner and he says nothing. He will get the full five years while you will walk free (with the trespassing charge dropped as a reward for your cooperation).
- Option B: You say nothing while your partner blames you for the theft. You will toil away inside for sixty long months while he's the one who will get off scot free.
- Option C: Neither of you says anything. The police charge both of you with trespass, and you both receive the maximum sentence of one year in prison.
- Option D: Out of mutual distrust, each of you dishes the dirt on the other. You both receive an intermediary term of three years inside.

What would you do?

Merrill Flood and Melvin Dresher dreamed up an abstract version of this scenario in 1950 – with Albert Tucker subsequently creating its dramatic prison setting – and it has since become a classic thought experiment in a branch of mathematics known as Game Theory[9]. Essentially, Game Theory attempts to model and understand patterns of conflict and cooperation between supposedly rational agents. Hence, the deep logic of the so-called 'prisoner's dilemma' has been applied to some of the most deadly and seemingly intractable problems in the world today. Why do countries continue to burn fossil fuels when they know we need to curb global emissions to put a brake on runaway climate change? Why do states spend vast proportions of their budgets on nuclear weapons that they will hopefully never use? The answer to both of these questions is that states which act unilaterally allow their rivals to reap the benefits of higher industrial output or extra military might. Everyone knows that the whole world would benefit if every country abolished its nuclear weapons and reduced its carbon emissions, but ongoing mutual distrust means that states continue to increase their nuclear stockpiles and allow their factories to keep polluting. They are being guided by their inner *Jewel Thiefs*, concerned only with short-term, selfish gain, regardless of the consequences.

Of course, we all need to look out for ourselves. Paradoxically, though, selfishness is often not in our best interests. In the prisoner's dilemma, for instance, you know that if both you and your accomplice remain silent and refuse to blame each other, you will each receive only one year in prison. But that runs the risk of your accomplice blaming you and walking away scot free while you serve five years. So you play it 'safe' and blame your accomplice, he does the same to you, and you both have to endure an extra two years inside. And governments adopt similar reasoning when discussing everything from carbon emissions to the arms race.

The invidious impact of selfishness is readily apparent closer to home, too. For instance, a healthy, loving relationship invariably requires reciprocal sacrifices: you postpone your bucket-list holiday to travel with your partner to their dream destination; they quit their job and you both move to a new city for the benefit of your career. This goes all the way down to the tiny details: you make breakfast so your partner can have a lie in; they wash up so you can relax afterwards. Successful relationships are forged in the intricate harmony of these little processes of give and take. Sometimes selfishness takes over, though. You suspect that doing a tiresome chore won't be noticed or appreciated, so you take the easy route and don't bother. This breeds resentment, and your partner responds by not cooking your favourite meal, as promised. Annoyed at the snub, you go out drinking with your mates. And so on . . .

These patterns will be familiar to anyone who has succumbed to selfishness – and that's all of us at one time or another. In such situations, *both* partners suffer, because life is altogether rosier when there is cooperation. Thankfully, though, guilt can play a redemptive role here. We are more likely to cooperate in the future if we dwell reflectively on our past selfishness, with the result that everyone wins. In this respect, Timothy Ketelaar and Wing Tung Au's exploration of the prisoner's dilemma is of particular interest.[10] Their experiment revealed that participants who were asked to reflect on a recent occasion when they had felt ashamed were far more cooperative than those who were not. In wanting to atone for their guilt, the former group avoided the selfish path we so often choose and instead took the higher road of cooperation.

So, feeling guilt over those times when we have listened to our inner *Jewel Thief* can be beneficial. It tends to make us better friends, better partners, better people. Studies have shown that a healthy sense of guilt is strongly associated with unselfish, relationship-enhancing behaviour – from a willingness to apologise, to 'learning lessons' and changing for the better.[11] Reflecting – in a self-compassionate way – on occasions when we've acted selfishly can help us avoid selfishness in the future. At other times, though, we may misbehave because of a desire to please *other* people.

The People Pleaser

You are employed in a vibrant, happy workplace. Everyone gets along fantastically well. You and your colleagues have developed dynamic relationships that generate great results for the company. There is good-natured banter around the water cooler, and you receive plenty of invitations to dinner parties and other social events that you are delighted to accept. In many respects, it is your dream job. But then something starts to nag away at you: you realise that not one of your colleagues seems to care about the environment. During the summer, the air-conditioning is constantly on full blast. Lights and computers are left on overnight. Reams of paper spool out of the printers before being scrunched up and thrown in the general direction of the overflowing bins. There is not even a hint of a recycling scheme. You are no militant environmental warrior, but this level of apathy really starts to bother you, so you tentatively mention your misgivings to a couple of colleagues by joking about paper not growing on trees. They manage a half-hearted chuckle but carry on regardless. Somewhat irritated, you press a bit harder. This time, one of your co-workers sighs, 'Oh, you don't need to worry about that here,' with a subtle undertone that implies, 'Drop it.'

What do you do? Continue to force the issue or forget it? After all, no crime has been committed; it's just another example of the casual carelessness and indifference that are so common in the world today. It would certainly be easier not to rock the boat. After all, no one likes the ghost at the feast, spoiling everyone else's day.

This is precisely how many misdeeds occur – not through the fear of punishment, or in the selfish pursuit of personal gain, but simply because we are reluctant to cause a fuss. It is the reasoning of the *People Pleaser*: we do whatever we can to fit in because we want to be the 'good boy/girl' who attracts approval. Most of us are familiar with the kind of dynamic described above, where going against the grain seems to be more hassle than it's worth. Indeed, we've all probably contributed to bad behaviour simply because of our desire to please people – whether actively (participating in something we know to be wrong) or passively (choosing not to speak out against such behaviour). If you are guilty of this, don't be *too* hard on yourself. The desire to be accepted, to be part of the group, can be extremely powerful. In fact, it is among the strongest of all motivating forces. Indeed, what kind of anti-social tyrant would you be if you did *not* wish to fit in, please people or feel accepted? Such behaviour is understandable and perfectly normal, and your sense of guilt for going along with the crowd may be out of proportion to what is merited.

At the same time, though, we do need to be careful of 'people pleasing', as it can get twisted in some extremely destructive ways. Roelie Mulder and colleagues showed how easy it is for employees to get sucked into the disturbing phenomenon of 'workplace mobbing' – essentially, bullying.[12] Say a junior member of staff is subjected to increasingly stigmatising behaviour from the powers that be. Their colleagues may initially rally to their defence (after all, most of us have a moral compass), but all too often self-interest wins out in the end. The bullied worker's colleagues want to retain the grace and favour of their bosses by presenting themselves as 'good employees' who don't cause trouble, even when they know they should. So, gradually, they stop speaking out on behalf of the victim. Apathy wins and we acquiesce to discrimination, even if we don't actively perpetrate it ourselves. Sometimes, though, we may go further and *join* the bullies at the heart of the mob.

I'm still mortified by a formative, shameful incident from my childhood. I was eight years old, and at my little primary school in West London. I was in a boisterous mood as I arrived just in time for the 9 a.m. bell, having dashed along the back streets from my home. As I sat down cross-legged on the linoleum floor, huddled with my gang of friends, suddenly we all got a whiff of a poisonous odour wafting through the air. Shock soon gave way to pantomime displays of disgust, and then, with a kind of gleeful cruelty, we focused on the most likely culprit – a boy who was often the target of taunting. Swept up disgracefully by the fever of the moment, I heckled him along with everyone else. But then the eyes of the boy next to me fell upon my own scruffy shoes. There, stuck to a heel, was a massive clump of dog dirt. *I* was the culprit. The derision instantly fell on my head, which was now burning with embarrassment. I can still recall in Technicolor detail the visceral sense of shame, and later a rising guilt at my collusion in the ridiculing of my innocent classmate.

In hindsight, though, I realise how valuable this shaming has been. Given my own taunting of an innocent party, my classmates' sudden, humiliating laughter was illuminating. Needless to say, the mockery felt dreadful at the time, but it had the just and beneficial effect of taking me down a peg or two. I'm not so bold as to claim that I've never participated in a collective misdeed since that day, but I was so chastened that I've always *tried* to refrain from taking any pleasure in the misfortune of others. (Sometimes I fail, of course, especially when my football team beats our rivals!) More generally, I've tried to remain cognisant of moments when I'm not being true to myself simply to gain the approval of a group. In that humbling childhood incident, I realised that I was liable to follow my inner *People Pleaser* ... and sometimes act reprehensibly because of it. This is valuable knowledge. It's great to be liked, and none of us wants to ruffle people's feathers just for the sake of it. But if we participate in (or simply acquiesce to) bad behaviour merely for the gratification of group approval, then we cheapen ourselves and abdicate our responsibility as moral agents.

In contrast, as we'll see in the following sections, standing up for principles can be both personally beneficial and meaningful. Such acts of conscience begin to emerge when we allow ourselves to be guided by our *Conscientious Rule Keeper*.

The Conscientious Rule Keeper

You're in a restaurant with a large group of friends, in fine spirits having just eaten your last, indulgent bite of a delicious lemon meringue pie. As you muse idly on whether to order a nightcap, you see the young couple at a nearby table working out the tip for their waiter. They search their pockets, deposit a number of coins on the table, then leave. Soon after, one of your party – more a tenuous acquaintance than a close friend – gets up to use the toilet, eases past the couple's vacated table, and casually picks up one of the pound coins. Blink and you would have missed it, as indeed everyone else has. You are the only one who noticed the nonchalant thief.

You're taken aback, but what do you do? You don't know the guy well, and he's breaking the law, but it's only a quid. Who cares? Is it worth kicking up a fuss and ruining a great night by creating a scene?

Let's play with the parameters. What if it wasn't a pound coin but a twenty-pound note? Or what if the couple had left a wallet on the table and the miscreant had helped himself to that? Surely such a level of criminality couldn't be overlooked. You like to think you would confront the guy, or at least alert the staff. But what if he wasn't some casual acquaintance but your best friend? What would you do then?

Adam Waytz and his colleagues have posed these sorts of scenarios to volunteers in their explorations of what is known as the 'whistle-blower's dilemma'.[13] This is the term for a conflict between two competing moral goods: loyalty and justice. On the one hand, most people would certainly consider loyalty a virtue. Yet it can place us in a difficult situation if the object of our loyalty engages in obvious wrongdoing. In such instances it compromises an innate sense of justice that seems to be almost hardwired into our psyches.[14] Our first instinct may be towards loyalty, but Waytz and his colleagues found that the scales eventually tip for most people – the moral calculation changes and our concern for justice starts to take precedence. This tipping point occurs at different points for each of us, since we all differ in the relative importance we attach to loyalty and justice. Other factors have roles to play too, including the severity of the crime and especially our closeness to the perpetrator. This latter factor can make it very hard to blow the whistle, as it will likely generate a strong sense of guilt *whatever* we decide to do.

Say a colleague at work has done something unethical and you are the only person who is aware of their misdeed. If you report them, that may lead to guilt over betraying a confidence, disrupting a friendship and ruining a career. Similarly, if the wrongdoing is more systemic – involving several people – you might be accused of disloyalty because of your refusal to play for the team. On the other hand, you would probably feel guilty if you did nothing and allowed the rules to be broken. After all, our systems of law and order are the structural foundations of civilisation, the supporting pillars that keep the whole edifice upright.

As with the other forms of guilt that are discussed in this chapter, your first priority should be to feel self-compassion. After all, through no fault of your own, you're damned if you do and damned if you don't. These kinds of moral dilemmas are hard, and it's unfair of someone else to land you with this burden. Whatever you decide to do, leaven any guilt you may feel with an understanding that you are just trying to do the right thing. Then, if you decide to speak out, you may be able to take solace and inspiration from others who have stood up for the rules. This path is rarely easy. Those who are brave enough to make a stand are often pilloried and punished, at least initially, but these dignified, committed individuals tend to be vindicated in the end. The truth will out . . . eventually. For instance, take the case of Jean Maria Arrigo.

Society appeared to unravel in the dark days following 11 September 2001, as if in a kind of collective nervous breakdown. Motivated by a dangerous cocktail of fury, desperation and grief, decent people began to contemplate doing bad things, such as torturing terrorist suspects to extract information and prevent future atrocities. Now, I'm not here to sit in judgement. I cannot imagine the burdens that must weigh on the shoulders of the people who are charged with keeping our nations safe. But over the last couple of centuries most civilised nations have decided that torture is an *absolute* wrong – not to mention generally ineffectual, since most people will admit to just about anything to stop the pain – and as such have enacted laws against it.

This new era of desperation and confusion left no area of life untouched, including the field of psychology. Enter Jean Maria Arrigo, who has devoted her long, illustrious career to the study of morality. In 2005, she was appointed to an ethics taskforce that oversaw the participation of psychologists in security interrogations. Arrigo's investigations led her to suspect that a number of psychologists were colluding in the mistreatment of suspected terrorists, despite their ostensible adherence to a strict ethical code that prohibits any sort of involvement in torture. So she began to speak out, initially within the taskforce itself and then more publicly. Life became hard. Some of her colleagues disbelieved her and accused her of causing unnecessary trouble. There were efforts to silence and ostracise her. But Arrigo persisted, certain of her facts. Finally, in 2015, there was some vindication: an authoritative report corroborated her suspicions, concluding that a number of psychologists had indeed collaborated in the introduction of torture practices.[15] With the report's publication, the field of psychology began an essential process of introspection, healing and returning to the right path. Indeed, in respect for Arrigo's vital role in this process, vindication was followed by recognition and gratitude: in 2016, the elite American Association for the Advancement of Science awarded Arrigo its prestigious Scientific Freedom and Responsibility Award.[16]

Through Arrigo's courageous efforts, her profession was reminded of the importance of abiding by rules – both legal and ethical – of which even the most thoughtful institutions can lose sight from time to time. Sometimes, though, the rules themselves are flawed, which leads us into the realm of the *Social Reformer*.

The Social Reformer

In this chapter, we've explored what motivates our behaviour and the various forms of guilt that might arise as a result. We may misbehave through fear of punishment (when we follow our inner *Obedient Servant*), through selfishness (the *Jewel Thief*) or because we seek approval (the *People Pleaser*); we may even feel guilty if we choose to uphold the law, for instance if doing so means hurting friends or colleagues who have done wrong (the *Conscientious Rule Keeper*). Moreover, we have begun to appreciate that these forms of guilt are not all 'equal' – some are better than others. Following the *People Pleaser* or the *Conscientious Rule Keeper* tends to yield both personal and objective benefits, whereas the *Obedient Servant's* or the *Jewel Thief's* guidance is usually detrimental. But the two 'higher' forms of motivation have their issues, too: for instance, people-pleasing may lead to collusion in bullying; and even conscientiously abiding by the rules can become problematic if those rules are flawed or immoral.

On 22 September 2015, the *Independent* newspaper gave the world a hard slap in the face. It took the almost unprecedented step of featuring on its front cover – in awful, vivid detail – the dead body of a child, washed up on a beach. For months, or even years, there had been vague murmurings throughout Europe about a 'migrant crisis' unfolding on the shores of the Mediterranean. The words 'Syria', 'boat people' and 'Greece' might surface occasionally in polite conversation, but the issue was not especially high on most people's agendas. This is not to accuse Westerners of heartlessness – most of us care about others – but we have own battles to fight, many of them close to home, and the problems in the Middle East were passing many of us by. But that front page really woke us up. We were suddenly forced to acknowledge that tens of thousands of desperate refugees – a modern-day exodus of biblical proportions – were fleeing mass slaughter and brutality and seeking a safe haven in Europe. The numbers were shocking enough, but it was the picture of three-year-old Aylan Al-Kurdi – who drowned when the dinghy that was transporting him and his family capsized off the coast of Turkey – that pricked the European consciousness and made the continent sit up and listen.

Just the previous month, David Cameron – in rather polemical, dehumanising terms – had warned of a 'swarm' of migrants arriving in the UK. Other European leaders had made similarly alarmist and hostile comments. International agreements were in place to keep the migrants out, so the *Conscientious Rule Keeper* would reason that most of the refugees should not be 'allowed' to enter Europe, since they weren't playing by the rules. But then almost the whole population of Europe suddenly seemed to realise that those rules were utterly inadequate for dealing with the unfolding catastrophe. The laws and conventions would need to be rethought, redrafted, rewritten. There was a collective shift among many people, signalling a widespread emergence of our inner *Social Reformers*. This was partly prompted by pragmatism: it was obvious that the old rules simply weren't working. How could strict quotas be maintained when the number of refugees dwarfed the figures that the law-makers had in mind when they drafted the statutes some years earlier? But far more important was the surge of collective guilt that the rules were simply *wrong*. Many people came to the conclusion that their *Conscientious Rule Keeper* – which urges adherence to the law at all times – was inadequate and inappropriate in this situation. In this instance, people didn't mind that the rules were being broken. In fact, any guilt they felt related to the rules themselves. Even while Europe continued to struggle with its own burdens of austerity, the heartbreaking images of thousands of haunted, desperate refugees generated astonishing displays of compassion and generosity. A fragile consensus started to emerge within Europe's conscience: we needed to do more to help. Of course, this wasn't unanimous – nothing ever is – but it would be fair to say that a majority chose to follow their inner *Social Reformer* rather than their *Conscientious Rule Keeper*.

Think of the German citizens who congregated at Munich's main train station to welcome the incoming refugees and applauded them off the carriages. Recall Nicola Sturgeon, Scotland's First Minister, offering a room in her own home to one migrant. Or consider the remarkable story of Rob Lawrie, the former soldier who dropped everything, hired a van, and started delivering food and clothes parcels to the thousands of refugees who were stranded within the refugee camp known as 'The Jungle' in Calais. Lawrie also comes to mind because he shows that, unfortunately, rules can be slow to change. In this instance, the emergent benevolent consensus

took time to translate into action as the politicians squab-
bled for national advantage, trying to reduce their countries'
respective obligations, while the refugees continued to suffer.
So people like Lawrie tried to help, often to their personal
cost. In the Calais camp, a man from Afghanistan pleaded
with him to smuggle his four-year-old daughter to relatives in
Leeds. Moved by paternal instinct, Lawrie – a father of four –
reluctantly agreed. He was caught at the border, arrested and
faced the real possibility of a five-year jail sentence (although
a sympathetic French judge eventually issued him with no
more than a suspended thousand-euro fine).

Rob Lawrie's example shows that we are sometimes com-
pelled to go beyond even the moralistic reasoning of the *Social
Reformer*. At such moments, we are guided by our *Principled
Idealist*.

The Principled Idealist

Dr Martin Luther King described following the highest level
of morality as becoming 'obedient to the unenforceable'.
We see this in the selfless, heroic actions of people like Rob
Lawrie. He did not run aid missions to The Jungle, or attempt
to rescue the Afghani girl, because someone ordered him to
and he risked punishment if he refused to obey. Nor did he
do so in a selfish quest for personal gain. (He presumably
felt a sense of pride and satisfaction, but these were surely
by-products of his altruistic actions, not the *cause* of them.)
Nor was he trying to please people in order to fit in. (There
are far easier and safer ways to gain social approval.) Nor did
the law of the land instruct him to behave as he did (quite

the contrary with respect to smuggling the little girl across the border). Nor were his actions even characteristic of the new European consensus. It is one thing to express concern for refugees and applaud them as they arrive in your city, but quite another to reorient your life to help them, put all of your effort into the cause, and risk your personal freedom for the sake of someone you have just met. Anyone who behaves in this way is following a deeper calling, abiding by an 'unenforceable' higher law.

Sometimes such a calling is religious in nature, inspired by the redemptive acts of a moral exemplar like Jesus or the Buddha. On other occasions it is guided solely by a sense of human decency and compassion, as appears to be the case with Rob Lawrie. But all such acts are united by the fact that they are genuinely *selfless*. Our usual preoccupation with ourselves is abandoned and replaced with a noble concern for the wellbeing of others. This is the highest form of guilt. People who attain this moral peak are not ashamed because they have behaved badly towards others, nor because they have failed to behave well. Rather, they are driven by a sense that – whatever good they may have done in the past – they could yet do more. Moreover, even if they reach the conclusion that they are doing everything they can – and so no longer suffer any personal guilt – they continue to feel guilty *on behalf of the rest of humanity*. They feel bad about the fact that people are suffering in the world – even if no one is to blame – and strive to help out of a sense of love and concern for others.

The general darkness of history is illuminated with many inspirational figures who far exceeded what was required or asked of them. They are testament to the incredible generosity of which the human spirit is capable. Some of them are

well known, such as Albert Schweitzer, the celebrated physician and theologian who cared for patients at the hospital
he founded in the middle of the Central African rainforest.
Others, like Sister Elvira Valentin Martin, are less famous
but no less remarkable. Born in Spain, in middle age Sister
Elvira felt compelled to travel to Taiwan and work in a san-
atorium. She remained there for the next forty years, caring
with selfless dedication for the hospital's bedridden lepers. In
2005, at the age of eighty-two, she received Taiwan's Medical
Dedication Award. When she was asked if she found the work
tiring, she replied: 'Not at all, because I love them.' There is
something very revealing in this reply. Looked at from the
outside, devoting one's life to the care of others might seem
unbearably punishing. We all know that even doing chores
can feel like a real hassle, so surely Sister Elvira's dedicated
service to others meant that she sacrificed her own happiness as a consequence? It seems that this was not the case,
however. Indeed, ancient wisdom and modern science both
suggest that compassion and especially caring for others can
lead to personal contentment.

The key to understanding this apparent paradox lies in the
notion of the 'self'. The modern world advocates aggrandise-
ment of our sense of self as a sure-fire route to happiness. Yet
all of the world's great religions – from Buddhism in the East
to Christianity in the West – teach that self-preoccupation
takes us in precisely the opposite direction. In fact, they view
the sense of self – and the understandable desire to protect
or reward it – as the very foundation of human suffering.
We spend our lives trying to defend this vulnerable fortress,
greedily grabbing anything that may shore it up and aggressively attacking anything that threatens it. But almost every

religious tradition suggests that we would be far more likely to find happiness – and maybe even transformative liberation – if we were to relinquish this frantic self-interest. And cultivating compassion for others is one of the most powerful ways to achieve this.

Scientific research is gradually starting to corroborate these ancient insights. Not that the world's great religions require scientific proof: every tradition can point to committed followers who have experienced the redemptive power of selflessness. That said, though, the more sceptical among us are certainly pleased to see scientific evidence pointing in the same direction. For instance, a number of experiments have found that compassion is associated with a spectrum of beneficial physical outcomes – from ameliorating the body's responses to stress,[17] to increased activity in the regions of the brain that generate positive sensations.[18] Moreover, it is possible to *practise* compassion. There is, for example, much empirical interest in the benefits of loving-kindness meditation, during which practitioners attempt to generate feelings of compassion. Having taught this technique to the employees of a software company, Barbara Fredrickson and her colleagues found that participants enjoyed significantly increased levels of positive emotion after just eight weeks of meditation. Moreover, this then had a transformative effect on other aspects of their lives, such as their personal relationships.[19]

Those inspirational figures who answer a higher calling and devote their lives to caring compassionately for others reveal just how redemptive this path can be. But we don't need to be an Albert Schweitzer or a Sister Elvira to start walking down it. This route to happiness is open to us all.

In this chapter, we've seen that we can harness guilt – in a considered and self-compassionate way – in order to become better people. We are making good progress if we start to follow our inner *People Pleaser* or *Conscientious Rule Keeper,* rather than our *Obedient Servant* or *Jewel Thief.* But at times we may be called to aim even higher. In such situations, we can strive to heed the advice of our *Social Reformer* or our *Principled Idealist.* The key point is that striving upwards not only improves our reputation in the eyes of others but enhances our personal wellbeing.

We will encounter a similar upward trajectory in the next chapter, where we learn how to harness envy in order to flourish and gain fulfilment.

CHAPTER FIVE

Envy

It's a grey Monday morning and you arrive at work to discover that an arrogant, ambitious colleague has been promoted ahead of you. Anger and resentment well up and are soon distilled into envy: you want what he has just got. Aggrieved, you hammer on your boss's door, demanding justice. Your boss patiently explains that, unbeknown to you, your rival recently attended an intensive training course, where he learned the precise skills that are needed for his new role, skills that you yourself lack. In a spirit of encouragement, your boss then suggests that you could take the same course – although she admits that it is very demanding and time-consuming – which would allow you to push for a similar promotion. You consider the suggestion, but then a malicious thought comes to mind. A few months back, your colleague committed a serious indiscretion that he confessed to you. If the story got out, it would certainly scupper his promotion and could even lead to dismissal. What do you do?

Work hard to raise yourself up to your colleague's new level, or fight dirty to drag him back down?

Encouragingly, when Giles Grolleau and his colleagues presented this scenario to participants in an experiment, only a minority said they would follow the latter option.[1] We might raise a sceptical eyebrow here and wonder if, in the real world, the majority would actually take the high road. Still, even taking into account the possibility that a number of the respondents were not entirely truthful – either with themselves or with the researchers – we can be confident that at least some people would use their envy to render themselves deserving of promotion and put in the necessary effort to reach that position.

Such studies have led to a re-evaluation of envy in the field of psychology. Indeed, it is becoming an increasingly prominent topic more generally, given its intimate connection to the dizzying and ever-growing world of social media. We are constantly bombarded with images of other people's supposedly perfect lives. Even though logic dictates that these images are hugely selective, their impact is powerful. We instinctively react, envious of what we don't have and jealous of people who seem to enjoy more money, better possessions, higher status, more exciting experiences, more loving relationships and greater happiness than us. Envy has risen dramatically in prominence as a societal concern as a direct result of this heightened exposure to other people's 'life highlights' over the last decade or so. At the same time, though, there have been suggestions that there are not one but two forms of envy – vicious and emulative – and they are very different.[2]

Vicious envy – as its name suggests – is invariably hostile

and corrosive. It is the simple resentment of another person's success that manifests in the desire to haul them down into the mud. By contrast, emulative envy is akin to admiration, comprising an altogether more uplifting mix of desire, longing and respect. If used wisely, this kind of positive envy can help us to clarify our goals and values, illuminate our path towards them and drive us forward to achieve them. In this sense, it is appropriate to speak of *moral* and even *spiritual* envy. For example, we look up to the Nelson Mandelas of this world and envy their moral strength and courage. This entails not only wishing that we could possess similar conviction and fortitude, but also attempting to follow in their esteemed footsteps.

Emulative envy is positive in two key respects. First, there is no resentment of the admired person's status and glory, and the envious party would certainly never wish to diminish or bring them down. Second, it is inspirational: it spurs us on to emulate our heroes by working hard to lift ourselves up to their exalted level. Indeed, for our envy to be positive, it *must* be emulative rather than vicious. As we saw in Chapter 3, if anger is not harnessed skilfully and thoughtfully, it can turn into a corrosive hatred that eats away at the soul. Vicious envy is a similarly insidious poison, gradually draining the world of all its joy and colour. Thus, envy should never be allowed to fester into resentment at others' success. This chapter will explain how such a destructive downward spiral can be avoided.

When envy first stirs within us, it is poised on a knife edge and can go either way: it might corrode into vicious envy, or rise up to emulative envy. The bad news is that it is all too easy to take the wrong path; the good news is that it is largely within our power to opt for the alternative. We can – and must – make a determined, conscious decision to choose emulative rather than vicious envy. There are two main ways in which we can do this. The first is to focus on ourselves, rather than on the target of our envy. Instead of obsessing over *their* good fortune, we work out what *we* can do to attain what they have. Hence, this chapter will explain how to develop this kind of focus, which involves drawing on envy as a motivational force to help us advance towards our goals.

But what if some of these goals are simply unattainable? For instance, I may envy the child with his whole life ahead of him, but I'll never be in that position again, no matter how hard I try. Similarly, despite my best efforts, I'm certain that I will never attain Bill Gates's wealth or David Beckham's footballing ability. It is precisely in this sort of situation, when disparity feels intractable – when it is *impossible* to bridge the divide – that envy is most liable to turn vicious. But there's a solution: in such circumstances we can work on the envy itself and turn it towards attaining more achievable outcomes. This is the second way of preventing envy from degenerating into viciousness. Moreover, we are helped by the serendipitous fact that these achievable goals tend to be more fulfilling than unfeasible objectives. Everything from better relationships to the cultivation of authenticity is within reach if we use envy wisely, and they are likely to be far more rewarding than the vast – and unattainable – riches that so many of us crave. So, as in the previous chapter – where we strove to develop 'better' forms of guilt – we can try to cultivate higher forms of envy by aiming for outcomes that are worthier and more deserving of our attention.

Reaching Higher

Abraham Maslow had a tough start in life. His parents fled Russia at the start of the twentieth century to escape the country's persecution of the Jews. They settled in the rough, working-class district of Brooklyn, where Maslow had to run the gauntlet of the violent, anti-Semitic gangs who roamed through the neighbourhood. He lifted weights in a bid to make himself more imposing, but found it hard to bulk up his slender frame. Thereafter, he found refuge in books and developed a deep, abiding passion for learning. He benefited from the guidance of a series of inspiring mentors, and eventually embarked on a career that would see him revolutionise the field of psychology. He was thirty-three, and the father of two small children, when the United States entered the war in 1941. Although ineligible for active service, he was shocked by the unfolding horror of this global conflagration. Rather than sinking into despair over the possible fate of the human race, though, he allowed himself to be guided by an urgent vision of peace.

The war was already revealing what can happen when human beings are at their worst. Certainly, the world needed to understand how the Nazis could sink to such a brutal nadir – and people like Stanley Milgram helped with that enquiry, as discussed in the previous chapter – but Maslow realised that we could approach the problem from the other direction, too. He started from the standpoint that most people are *not* evil, violent or sadistic, but are generally kind and decent. Then, setting his sights higher still, Maslow focused his attention on his mentors – the groundbreaking anthropologist Ruth Benedict and the Gestalt psychologist Max Wertheimer, two extraordinary people for whom Maslow's respect and admiration were total, whom he regarded as beacons of love, peace and reason. How do such people turn out so *well*, he wondered?

This question led Maslow to embark on a quest to understand human potential. Legions of scientists were trying to fix humanity's tragic flaws, but almost no one was asking the equally important question of how we might help people flourish and reach their respective peaks of development and fulfilment. As Maslow said, in reference to Sigmund Freud's epochal research into neuroses, 'It is as if Freud supplied us the sick half of psychology and we must now fill it out with the healthy half.'[3] In so doing, Maslow founded the field of 'humanistic psychology', radically reshaping our concept of what human beings can become.

He formulated many beautiful ideas in his long and highly distinguished career, but he is perhaps best known for his notion of the 'hierarchy of needs'. This idea has since become one of the most influential in all psychology. Maslow argued that human beings have a core set of needs that must be satisfied if we are to be happy and well. This was not a particularly new idea, but Maslow's genius was to see that such needs could be arranged in a hierarchy.[4] At the base are our lower-level needs: to be safe, fed, secure and so on. These are not depicted as 'lower' because they are less important than the others. On the contrary, they lie at the base of the pyramid because they are our most fundamental needs – the foundations of the whole structure. Without them, it would be very hard – although still possible – to reach the higher levels. But once these basic needs are met, we are empowered to proceed up the hierarchy. This process is unsettling and exciting in equal measure.

It is unsettling because a higher goal invariably appears just when we think we've attained everything we could ever need or desire. So we are obliged to keep moving upwards. It can be tiring, but it also makes life exciting. As our lower-level needs are satisfied, we are compelled to give ever more time, thought and energy to more elevated goals, more rarefied values. These may not be more *important* than the lower-level needs, but achieving them is certainly more *fulfilling*. Think of climbing a high mountain. The first few steps are just as essential – if not more so – than the final stride onto the summit. But that last step is the one that provides the glorious panorama.

We can use Maslow's theory to help us understand the transformative power of envy. In particular, we shall see that emulative envy is a powerful motivating force that can propel us up through all six hierarchical levels. The first level comprises our physiological needs – the fundamental necessities that must be met if we are to remain alive: food, water, oxygen, warmth, sleep. If we lack any of these essentials, we will surely envy those who possess them. In this chapter, we shall personify this aspect of envy as the *Life Giver*, which pushes us to obtain the basics of life. Once we've met those needs satisfactorily – or at least are making good progress towards them – we can set our sights on the next step, safety, which comprises our need for security and stability. Here, envy can serve as our inner *House Builder*, pushing us towards establishing safety and order in our lives.

With these essentials in our grasp, or at least within reach, a new tranche of needs comes to the fore, demanding our attention. First, there is the need for love and belonging. Of course, this matters to all of us, irrespective of whether our physiological and safety needs have been met. But the key point is that our need to belong and to feel loved becomes *dominant* – our overriding concern – as soon as the lower-level concerns have been addressed. Consequently, at this level, envy may be personified as our inner *Love Seeker*, driving us to seek communion and connection with others. Once we have attained these noble goals, the journey continues. The security that we find in belonging and feeling loved can become a platform for the next level: esteem. Our priorities are now to be valued and respected for our achievements. Here, envy becomes our *Self Striver*, pushing us to make something of ourselves. Motivated by our heroes and heroines, we aspire towards ever greater attainment and success.

Once these glittering goals are in reach, we are tempted to push even further, to the level of self-actualisation. Here, our chief concern is no longer with worldly achievement or garnering plaudits for our success. Rather, we set about discovering who we really are, deep down, and reaching our full potential. Envy now becomes our *Pathfinder*, guiding us to our true destiny and the higher realms of human achievement. But then the path goes even higher, into the mysterious, misty peaks of the sacred. Here we encounter the 'spiritual envy' of our inner *Soul Shaper*, which propels us towards self-transcendence. Before ascending these distant summits, though, we need to start at the beginning and take our first vital steps up the mountain.

The Life Giver

Most people love a good rags-to-riches tale. They are the stuff of dreams, inspirational quotes and sepia-tinged Hollywood films. We are usually captivated not by the acquisition of a vast fortune per se, but by the hero or heroine's capacity to advance through sheer hard work, determination and a fair sprinkling of luck. The heart of such narratives lies in the protagonist's circumstances before success is even glimpsed, right back at their lowest ebb. Think of Jan Koum, the founder and CEO of WhatsApp, which Facebook recently acquired for a mind-blowing $19 billion. Koum grew up in a poor Ukrainian village before emigrating to California with his mother and grandmother when he was sixteen years old. At first, the family relied on social welfare and food stamps. Or Ursula Burns, chairwoman and CEO of Xerox, the first African-American woman to lead a Fortune 500 company, and the twenty-second most powerful woman in the world, according to *Forbes* magazine. She was raised by her mother in an impoverished New York social housing project. Or Dhirubhai Ambani, one of India's most successful business-men and the patriarch of the world's second-richest family, who according to legend had only a single rupee to his name when he started out.

We might well marvel at these people, and indeed be envious of their success. But the crucial point is that they all inspire *emulative* envy. Their stories are testament to the possibility that we could better ourselves, too; not by tearing other people *down* in a fit of vicious envy, but by raising our-selves *up* through sheer grit and determination. Moreover, we can appreciate that these icons were probably driven by their own feelings of emulative envy, which pushed them to follow in the footsteps of their idols. For, while their stories may seem like fabulous fairy tales, think what life must have been like for them when they were truly hard-up, toiling on the margins of society, battling through poverty and social insecurity. Merely emerging from such beginnings without falling into the pitfalls that can attend social deprivation – from ill health to poor job prospects – is admirable enough. But they then went on to succeed beyond most people's wildest dreams through sheer strength of will.

I'm not suggesting that Koum, Burns and Ambani are exemplars of jealousy. Their respective recollections about their upbringings betray no sense of bitterness or resentment at the success of others. Rather, they all epitomise the drive to improve *their own* situations. Struggling through their youths, they surely gazed longingly at those who were already enjoying the fruits of successful lives and careers. But – as far as I know – they never wished such people ill or sought to haul them down. Instead, they put all their energy and talents into raising themselves up. This is the very definition of emulative envy, and it is a million miles away from the vicious variety.

Such positive envy may be far more common than we realise. Niels van de Ven asked volunteers to recall their experiences of envy and found that its beneficial – emulative – form accounted for around 40 per cent of their memories.[5] His project also revealed the vast gulf that separates the two types of envy. Participants who remembered feeling the vicious form tended to exhibit bitterness and hatred. In contrast, those who recalled emulative envy seemed to be enthused, energised and inspired by the memory. This tallies with what we know about the Herculean efforts of our three exemplars: it would surely be impossible to undertake such ambitious and far-reaching journeys without a powerful motivational force driving you on.

But this chapter is not merely about famous luminaries

who have risen to the peaks of their professions. The world is full of millions of unsung heroes whose achievements are no less spectacular, in their own ways. Such people are no less dedicated, no less driven to create better lives for themselves and their families. They also exemplify the tremendous power of emulative envy as a *Life Giver*, a motivational resource that helps us fight to secure the necessities that keep us alive. Consider the hundreds of millions of parents across the globe who struggle to provide warmth, food and medicine for their children. They may envy the affluent classes who live in gated communities on the other side of town – and surely wish that they too could enjoy a life of ease and comfort – but this envy drives them forward in a positive way. They fight to do all they can to reach this goal through their own valiant efforts. Or consider the generations of migrants – including Abraham Maslow's own parents – who have endured untold hardships in the search for more prosperous futures. Among their number are the desperate refugees who are currently fleeing the Middle East, whose tragic tale we told in the previous chapter. Theirs is partly a flight *from* suffering, horror and war, but it is also a brave quest *for* survival and prosperity. They are not driven by the kind of superficial, resentful envy that covets an easy life, as some tabloids would have us believe. Rather, they have a deep, primal desire to safeguard their families by securing the essentials of life. It is this instinct that keeps them alive.

So, emulative envy can serve as a *Life Giver*, pushing us to gain the fundamentals of existence through sheer resolve. Sometimes, though, hard work is not enough: no matter how hard we try, the game seems rigged against us. This involves more than being dealt a bad hand. Our opponent – dressed in his opulent finery – is not only friends with the dealer but has written the rules himself to ensure that he cannot lose. In other words, society is all too often weighted in favour of the rich, the privileged. Look at the fiscal rules in Britain and the United States, which penalise the rich far less than the so-called 'precariat' – those workers who toil for little reward and lack any sort of job security, such as the people who clean the upper classes' mansions for pennies. Since the crash of 2008, the richest thousand families in the UK have seen their aggregate net worth double to £547 billion, while the poorest members of society have become 57 per cent worse off.[6] These statistics – so stark in their unfairness – are shocking and understandably generate resentment. The wealthy often attempt to dismiss such complaints as the 'politics of envy' – as if everyone else were simply jealous of their 'success'. In one sense they're right, because there is envy here. But it is more an emulative envy for the kind of society we *could* have – one that is fairer and more humane. This brings us to the second level in Maslow's hierarchy: the *House Builder.*

The House Builder

Every time you see a chart of the happiest countries in the world, or the healthiest, or the most socially connected, the chances are that Scandinavian nations will dominate the top ten. Take the World Happiness Report – the gold-standard assessment of contentment – which is produced by some of the world's foremost economics, psychology and social policy experts. In 2016, the five Nordic countries occupied positions one, three, four, five and ten.[7] And this was no fluke – they've appeared in the top ten ever since the index was first published in 2011. The research has a relatively simple methodology. Across the world, people are asked to rate the quality of their lives on a scale of 0 to 10. Zero is the worst life imaginable – hell on Earth – while 10 would be the best conceivable existence, paradise gained. All of the responses from each country are then averaged to produce its overall quality of life. And so it was that the ten happiest countries in the 2016 report were, in order: Denmark, Switzerland, Iceland, Norway, Finland, Canada, Holland, New Zealand, Australia and Sweden. These all had scores in the spectacularly high realm of 7–8, which is light years away from the devastatingly low scores of the nations at the bottom of the pile: Benin (3.48), Afghanistan (3.36), Togo (3.30), Syria (3.06) and tragic Burundi (an almost unimaginable 2.90).

The obvious conclusion is that the happiest countries are also the richest, while the most miserable are riven by grinding poverty. This logic does indeed make some sense, particularly given the importance of meeting our basic, physiological needs, as detailed earlier. If your country is scrabbling around at the bottom, struggling to provide the necessities that people need to stay alive, then an influx of cash can be a great help (provided that it is equitably distributed and not greedily snatched by those in power). Those who say that money can't buy you happiness are wrong ... up to a point at least. Money can buy food, clothes and medicine, which in turn can alleviate the spectres of illness, starvation and death. Any country that manages to do that will surely rise up the happiness scale.

But once those essentials are secured – whether individually or for a whole society – simply acquiring more of them ceases to have a significant effect on happiness. The difference between starving and eating regularly – or, to put it another way, the difference between living and dying – is effectively infinite; but thereafter, having access to a banquet of choice does not make us any happier. Indeed, as Barry Schwartz has found, too much choice can be overwhelming and may even make us more miserable.[8] (We'll return to this in the chapter on boredom.) The economist Richard Easterlin was the first to notice this – at the time unexpected – pattern in the 1970s.[9] Although countries like the USA and the UK were growing richer year on year, their populations were no happier than they had been previously. This phenomenon became known as the 'Easterlin Paradox',[10] but of course it seems paradoxical only because we have been indoctrinated by a century of clever advertising and manipulative politicians who have managed to convince us that that riches equal happiness. As I said earlier, this equation does indeed hold true for extremely poor countries (and people): as they secure life-giving necessities, their happiness rises. But once such countries reach a level of prosperity where most of the population can afford most of the basic necessities most of the time, any extra money has no particular impact on their happiness.

At this point, the most important factor becomes the *distribution* of the money. This was precisely why Maslow devised his hierarchy of needs. Once the physiological basics are covered, other issues – such as law and order, universal education and welfare provision – start to matter more. Above all – as Richard Wilkinson and Kate Pickett have demonstrated so persuasively – a society's level of *equality* is the principal determinant of its wellbeing.[11] The more unequal a society (the bigger the gap between rich and poor), the worse it does on just about every metric available: mental health, crime rate, level of trust, educational performance. Moreover, it's not just the poor who do badly in these societies. *Everyone* takes a hit, including the rich. Of course, they can insulate themselves, to some extent, by hiding within gated communities and paying for private healthcare. But they still have to drive down streets that are heavy with fear and mistrust and lack real connection between the people. As John F. Kennedy once said, 'If a free society cannot help the many who are poor, it cannot save the few who are rich.' So, we would be wise not only to envy the Scandinavians' greater happiness, but, more importantly, to emulate the reasons for that happiness.

Their formula is simple: they perform so well in the well-being league tables because they are much more equal than the likes of the USA and the UK (which have comparable wealth). They have reined in the inequality that is generated through free-market capitalism by imposing high taxes and establishing strong welfare states. If society were a house, the Nordic countries have done a better job of building theirs. There are no gilded chambers for a privileged elite while the majority are forced to huddle together in squalid rooms with crumbling walls and cracked windows. In this house the rich help to maintain the quarters of the poor, and everyone has enough to get by.

The lesson here is that we, as a society, need to build a better house – and we can find the motivation to do so in our emulating envy of the Scandinavians' superior dwellings.

There's no point tearing down their houses (as vicious envy might be inclined to do); rather, we should work together to build something similar for ourselves. So, at this level of Maslow's hierarchy – the need for a safe and prosperous community – we must get involved and help to improve our society. We might do this quite simply through the electoral process. After all, it is within our democratic power to vote and indeed campaign for candidates who advocate a more equal society. Or we could be more proactive and offer our time, enthusiasm and skills to a worthwhile cause, such as a local charity.

Then, once we are working towards a better society, we can turn our sights to the next level: the *Love Seeker*.

The Love Seeker

It's not just about the house. Having a strong, well-maintained structure that provides shelter for everyone inside is vital. But then what really starts to matter is how those people treat each other. The previous level of the *House Builder* referred not merely to keeping ourselves alive by addressing our physiological needs but also to cultivating a prosperous and equitable society that meets our safety and security concerns. We all benefit from a society in which we are guarded from crime (a good police force and a fair legal system), supported when we're weak or out of luck (strong welfare provision) and so on. But is that enough? What about those moments that light up our days – a kiss from a loved one, a kind word from a colleague, a smile from a stranger? What if we can't trust our neighbours, have no friends to lean on or find work drudgery because we don't get along with our colleagues? To explore these questions, we shall revisit Scandinavia. This time, though, the discussion will be more than a straightforward celebration of the region; because, even in these pinnacles of civilisation, there are some remarkable differences in health and happiness. And many of these can be traced back to the *Love Seeker*: our need to belong and to be loved.

In the early years of this century, Markku Hyyppä and Juhani Mäki conducted a landmark study on the cold western coast of Finland.[12] Nestled within the Finnish-speaking majority of the region is a Swedish-speaking minority, a legacy of the seven centuries during which Finland was ruled by its western neighbour. Other than this linguistic difference, though, the two groups are very similar. They share almost identical genetic profiles, physical constitutions, levels of educational attainment, job prospects, socio-economic status, access to services (such as healthcare) and so on. To use the metaphor of the previous level, the two groups share a single house. Their ecological context is identical too, of course: they breathe the same air, eat the same fish, look up at the same stars. Yet the members of the Swedish-speaking minority tend to live far longer than their Finnish-speaking compatriots – fully eight years longer in the case of the men. So what is going on?

After analysing the two groups' behavioural patterns, Hyyppä and Mäki felt that the difference in life expectancy can be explained by a single factor, namely 'social capital'. We're all familiar with the concept of *economic* capital: the money in our bank accounts, the financial resources that allow us to buy what we need and splash out on what we want. Similarly, social capital is the sum total of our *social* resources: the number of people we know and feel we can turn to for help, the degree of trust we have in our neighbours, the extent to which we feel part of our community, the quality of our friendships, the number of communal activities in which we participate, the depth of the love we receive from those who are close to us and so on. While all of the participants in Hyyppä and Mäki's study enjoyed comparable levels of (high) economic capital, the Swedish-speakers appeared to have far greater social capital. During interviews, they were much more likely to dwell on themes of relationships, attachment, reciprocity and affiliation. In life, they tended to join more social clubs and voluntary organisations, spent more time connecting with friends, and in general felt a far stronger sense of community. These patterns of behaviour seemed to benefit their health in two significant ways – they were not only physically fitter than their Finnish-speaking neighbours but had more sources of support to help them through times of stress. They were also happier, which is hardly surprising as they were much more likely to meet the third of Maslow's hierarchy of needs: the need to belong and to feel loved.

So, who should we envy? The wealthy person laden with riches and material possessions, or the one who is blessed with abundant social capital? Well, if we're struggling to survive, if our fundamental physiological and safety needs are not being met, then of course we must amass the economic capital we need to stay alive and well. But, once these needs are satisfied, we would be well advised to elevate our concerns and set our sights higher, because accumulating ever more possessions and wealth will not necessarily make us any happier. At this point, our overriding need is for community and belonging. We should envy the sociable Swedish-speaking Finns.

More to the point, we should harness this envy in an emulative and constructive way by using it as our motivational *Love Seeker*. This does not entail forlornly thinking that the only way to find happiness is to be romantically 'in love'. Rather, it means recognising the value of participating and being part of something. There are so many ways to connect, socialise and build bridges with other people in our communities. Whatever your hobby, however you like to spend your time – from salsa, to chess, to skydiving – there will be a group of like-minded people who come together to enjoy that activity. In many ways, the activity itself is merely a good excuse to make new friends. For instance, a friend of mine founded a knitting group that meets in local pubs (hence its name: the Drunken Knitwits). Sometimes I tag along, even though I can't knit (so I am officially a 'half-wit'), just to enjoy a pint with an interesting group of people. We all know that striking up new friendships can be hard, particular as we get older. We're unlikely to stride up to a stranger in a pub and brazenly introduce ourselves (especially if we're English). So these kinds of clubs serve the very useful purpose of facilitating the much-needed introductions in a structured and friendly way. They are specifically designed to bring people together.

I should add that there is no need to necessarily try to become the life and soul of the party when joining a new social group; and it's also fine to spend some time on your own. We all have a certain level of sociability, and a counterbalancing degree of introspection, which feels natural and right for us (as we shall see in the chapter on loneliness).

Sometimes, though, we need a little prompting to break out of our shells, peer over our defensive walls, and reach out to the people on the other side. Moreover, a sense of belonging provides a secure platform from which we can climb even further up Maslow's hierarchy of needs. Plant your feet on the solid ground and then launch yourself up to the next level, where the *Self Striver* is waiting to guide you.

The Self Striver

I first encountered the painful reality of the *Self Striver* during a rather dark, murky time in my life. It is at this level of Maslow's hierarchy that our need to be respected as a worthwhile person and rewarded for our endeavours becomes paramount. But just after leaving university, all of my plans seemed to evaporate, like the moment when dreams scatter upon waking and you are left clutching at half-remembered fragments. In this difficult period I began to appreciate the deep-seated need we all have for esteem, mainly because I felt rather lacking in this respect, being at a rather self-pitying, low ebb. Yet I also started to understand how emulative envy can help us to meet this need. First, though, it bears stressing that esteem is also important to those who are struggling to meet the 'lower-level' needs of physiological necessity, safety and belonging. A lonely, homeless man who is fighting just to stay alive obviously needs – and deserves – to be treated with dignity and respect. But this will not necessarily become his main focus until his more fundamental needs are met.

These notions were brought home to me through a series of

events that, in retrospect, helped set the future course of my life. Throughout university, much to the consternation of my tutors, I was captivated by the whirl of the local music scene, where I formed my weird and wonderful ska band. Caught up with the excitement of playing live, it was only my parents' wise counsel that stopped me from dropping out of university altogether and focusing full time on the band. Nevertheless, upon graduation, my plan was to concentrate on 'making it' in the music industry. Then, a few months later, it all came crashing down. We had spent much of the summer in a studio working on our first album, but near the end of that process we fell out with our manager, and the whole project stumbled to a halt, never to resume. The wind was taken completely from our sails, and the band fell apart.

The worst part of this scenario was that I didn't have a back-up plan. Most of my classmates were already embarking on exciting new adventures – from lucrative graduate jobs, to round-the-world trips. But I had been so caught up in the luminous promise of the band that I suddenly felt stranded. It was at this moment that envy began to seep into my soul. I had previously suffered moments of jealousy – looking longingly at people who seemed to possess some advantage or talent that I lacked – but now these comparisons reached a new level. Mercilessly, and with damning judgement, I found myself wanting in many aspects of life. My peers were all sailing merrily off into rosy, prosperous futures, while I was marooned on my desolate island, having missed the boat. They were building promising careers, while I was working for the minimum wage as a psychiatric nursing assistant.

I had a complicated relationship with this job. On the one

hand, I still harboured vague hopes of forging a career in psychology, maybe as a therapist, and I knew that nursing would provide a solid foundation of experience. Moreover, I found the work very fulfilling. As I mentioned in the chapter on sadness, there were even moments – perhaps sitting with a patient in the unearthly stillness of the evening – that felt almost sacred in their significance. At the same time, though, it was physically and especially mentally arduous work. And, more troublingly, I felt insignificant, a failure.

In this self-pitying mood, I envied most people I knew in one way or another. But then I began to notice that this unpalatable emotional brew contained some surprisingly nourishing nutrients. For a start, my envy clarified what I felt was lacking in my life. It provided the self-knowledge that let me understand what I truly valued. This self-awareness was not always pleasant: for instance, I realised that, contrary to what I told myself, I coveted status and recognition. But when I focused on *who* I envied, I gained a clearer sense of direction. I wasn't particularly jealous of classmates who had entered the yawning maw of the City or a dizzying, fast-track graduate-training scheme. Rather, I envied those peers who were making headway in the field of psychology. As such I felt that this was my road too, even though I'd fallen some way behind. I took comfort from the fact that at least I now had a sense of where I wanted to go. Moreover, I learned how to harness my emulative envy, which gave me the motivation I needed to catch up. I resolved to work all the harder and started studying alone in order to gain a postgraduate research position. It was five years before I was granted that opportunity, partly because, in a strange twist of fate, the band reformed and took off, captivating my attention once again. Nevertheless, throughout those five years, my admiration – my envy – for my peers in psychology continued to be a guiding light, steering me towards the career that I would eventually pursue.

So, our envy can push us to work hard for the recognition and respect we crave, helping us to become *Self Strivers*. And yet, even as we start to achieve some recognition and a measure of esteem, we may begin to see beyond this type of external validation. It's not that the respect of others ceases to matter. It's more that previously concealed needs begin to assume greater significance. Here we meet the *Pathfinder*.

The Pathfinder

Who do you most admire? I'm not just talking about people who have achieved notable successes in their fields or even those who have found contentment in their lives. That type of admiration belongs at the level of the *Self Striver*. Instead, try to think of someone who simply seems to exist on a higher plane than everyone else. They see farther, think quicker, walk taller. They judge with more wisdom, speak with more clarity, move with more grace. Maslow himself revered a host of illustrious names, beacons who not only illuminated their own fields of endeavour – Einstein revolutionising science, Beethoven composing music for the ages, Lincoln transforming politics – but transcended those fields by offering their gifts to the world. He eulogised Lincoln, for instance, not merely as a great politician but as a great man – indeed, one of the greatest who has ever lived. Each of these people seemed to reach a peak of human development.

It was not necessarily because they were clever, or skilful or brave. It was more that their unique qualities and experiences combined to produce singular characters of genuine nobility. Maslow called them 'self-actualisers': people who had actualised (or realised) their full potential.

I felt something of the admiration Maslow reserved for his luminaries when I first heard Barack Obama speak. I was awestruck, filled with approbation that only increased during his thrilling election campaign. His inspirational speeches captivated not only Americans, who yearned to heal the bitter divides that were fracturing their nation, but a worldwide audience who longed for hope and change. Sure, he was aided by speech-writers and soaring oratory, but it was not the words he used or the eloquence of his delivery that made him so impressive. Something about the man himself seemed truly great, as if he were cut from a finer cloth than the rest of humanity. Don't get me wrong, I know that he's not perfect; and, like many others, I've been disappointed by aspects of his presidency. But, in my eyes, his policy failures don't really diminish Obama himself. After all, he's only human, and he's done his utmost in unimaginably complex situations and within the constraints of an intransigent political system. If he's let anyone down, it's probably because we loaded too many burdens and expectations on his shoulders. I still regard him as an exemplary human being, a model of how good a man can be.

This brings us to the emulative envy of the *Pathfinder*. At this level of the hierarchy, we are not overly concerned with possessions (the envy of the *Life Giver*), security (the envy of the *House Builder*), a sense of belonging (the envy of the *Love Seeker*), or achieving recognition (the envy of the *Self Striver*).

Rather, we envy – or admire – our heroes and heroines as *people*. If harnessed correctly, this emulative envy can motivate us to follow in their footsteps and ascend to their lofty heights. We see where they are – in terms of character and moral purpose – and we are driven to climb up and join them. That's why, at this stage of development, envy is our *Pathfinder*. It illuminates the road we should take and urges us to follow it. But this is not a matter of *copying* our hero's destination. While we may wish to emulate their admirable qualities and traits – such as Obama's graceful intelligence and cool poise – our aim should not be to develop in exactly the same way. Rather, we must endeavour to discover and fulfil our *own* potential. As the iconoclastic writer Kurt Vonnegut wrote to a class of high-school children, 'Practice any art, music, singing, dancing, acting, drawing, painting, sculpting, poetry, fiction, essays, reportage, no matter how well or badly, not to get money and fame, but to experience becoming, to find out what's inside you, to make your soul grow'.[13]

This is important, because otherwise we can get preoccupied with achieving particular outcomes and judge ourselves harshly if we fall short. Becoming president of the United States is a one in a billion shot. So, if we were to appraise our own success according to this impossibly high bar, we would inevitably fall short. Indeed, this level of the hierarchy is not really about 'achievements'; such concerns belong to the level of the *Self Striver*. Instead, the *Pathfinder* is more about flourishing as a person, regardless of whether this leads to accolades and acclaim. When asked what he would have been had he not become a boxer, Muhammad Ali replied: 'I'd have been a bin-man ... [but] I'd have been the best bin-man in the world.' That may sound like braggadocio, but to my mind he was just saying that he would have embraced whatever hand fate had dealt him, and he would have done so with *style*.

Ali's philosophy no doubt inspired many thousands of people to follow *their* destinies with heart and style. They didn't necessarily dream of becoming boxers, just as Obama's supporters do not necessarily dream of becoming politicians. But such inspirational figures embolden the rest of us to take the next step on the path to becoming the best people we can be. Take Maxi Jazz, lead vocalist of the group Faithless. He raps of seeing his hero Ali fight on TV and the self-belief that gave him as he fended off racism on the hard streets of seventies Brixton. Then, years later, he harnessed that precious confidence to pursue his musical dreams.

Even as we are empowered to tread our own unique paths, though, we may begin to realise that it's not all about us. At this point, we are approaching the highest level of Maslow's hierarchy: the realm of the *Soul Shaper*.

The Soul Shaper

Have you ever enjoyed a moment in your life when everything seemed absolutely perfect? I don't just mean a time when all your boxes seemed to be ticked – you're in love, your work is going swimmingly, all of your friends and family are in good health, and you're lying on the golden sands of a tropical beach drinking a mai tai. Rather, I'm talking about one of those extraordinary instants when the universe seems utterly illuminated and transformed. You feel as though you've shifted to a higher plane of reality where everything seems to make sense. The world is captivating in its beauty, the very embodiment of love. *You* don't really matter any more. Your life, with all of its troubles and concerns, has been quietly forgotten, replaced with a sense of awe at the grandeur of life itself. These moments can materialise at any time, perhaps when you are trudging along the street to work. But they are more likely to descend upon us when we escape our normal, everyday routine – perhaps when we stand atop a mountain peak, high above the world, breathless from the exhilarating climb. This was why Maslow called such moments 'peak experiences'. They stand out from the rest of life like some experiential Everest, living for ever in the memory as glimpses of perfection, true highlights of existence.

Maslow gradually became aware of a paradox as he pondered these peak experiences. He realised that when people reach this peak of personal fulfilment they also seem to go *beyond* themselves: the self appears to drop away, forgotten. This may all sound rather mystical – and indeed it is – but it is not some supernatural weirdness. Someone who experiences these peaks still knows that they are a person with a name, a history, an identity. But they see these cognitive 'facts' as unimportant because they suddenly realise that their being is far larger than they had ever suspected. It is akin to a drop of water that enters the ocean. The droplet may remain intact on a molecular level, but at the same time it becomes one with the limitless expanse all around it. Hence, Maslow argued that self-actualisation is both a destination – a 'culmination' of the self – *and* the start of a whole new transcendental journey *beyond* the self. Of course, he was not the first person to dwell on this notion of self-transcendence, or to recognise that it can be the doorway to the most elevated states that a human being may experience. Every spiritual tradition has understood this for thousands of years. And they are all united by a common thread – namely, that the spiritual seeker aims to cultivate a form of experiential union with the focus of their reverence. This is why Christians pray and Buddhists meditate: they are attempting to transcend the self and become one with something infinitely grander and more beautiful than themselves.

It is for this reason that we may speak of *spiritual* envy. All through our life journey, we are propelled forward by emulative envy. If we lack the fundamentals to sustain life, such as food and shelter, our inner *Life Giver* can motivate us to obtain them. Then, once we have all we need, there is little point in trying to accumulate more, as doing so will not make us any happier. Rather, we might start to envy people who enjoy stronger communities and closer relationships, letting ourselves be guided by our internal *House Builder* and *Love Seeker* to attain such advantages for ourselves. Then, as we start to envy other people's success, the *Self Striver* can exhort us towards higher personal achievement, while our admiration of inspirational figures can serve as a *Pathfinder*, galvanising us to fulfil our potential. Having reached that point, though, we may realise that we can aim higher still. Even if we become self-actualised, we do not have to rest on our laurels. There are still exemplars to revere and emulate. It is when we understand this that we start to experience spiritual envy.

I believe this is one reason why so many people are drawn to religious and spiritual traditions. At the heart of each of these is a rare jewel, a world-shaping human being, around whom the tradition has crystallised. Ever since these figures walked the earth, millions of devotees have tried to follow in their footsteps, guided by a transformative sense of emulative envy. For instance, they might envy the love and compassion of Jesus, or the wisdom and insight of the Buddha. This envy is emulative in the sense that the followers hope, pray and endeavour to become as loving and wise as their spiritual leaders.

This 'higher' form of envy is valuable for many reasons, not least because it prevents the 'lower' forms of envy from corroding into viciousness. As I mentioned at the start of the chapter, no matter how hard we try, we will never accumulate as many riches and achievements as some of our idols. And if our efforts to emulate them fall persistently short, there is certainly a risk of our envy turning vicious. If that happens, however, we need only raise our sights and aim for the higher forms of envy. Indeed, striving for the highest level – the spiritual envy of the *Soul Shaper* – may be the most potent remedy of all. While we may never attain a great fortune or spectacular success, it is always within our power to be more loving and compassionate. Furthermore, if we cannot match the superhuman qualities of our religious exemplars, we can at least try to journey towards them.

Envying others who are further down that road is also helpful in keeping us on the right track. I often used to attend one particular Buddhist centre. There I was struck by how the newer members not only revered the Buddha as their principal guiding example but also tried to emulate the more senior figures within the community. Yet you do not have to be religious – or even consider yourself particularly spiritual – to benefit from the spiritual envy of the *Soul Shaper*. I know plenty of resolute atheists who find the Pope or the Dalai Lama inspirational. Following their example may help you, too. And if you allow yourself to be guided, you may be blessed with precious moments of self-transcendence. These peak experiences can transform our lives and help us to view them in a new, glowing light.

We may also find self-transcendence in entirely unexpected quarters, as we shall see in the next chapter, where we explore the strange magic at the heart of boredom.

CHAPTER SIX

Boredom

Your train is already late when the announcer 'regrets to inform you' that it will be delayed for another hour. Already you begin to feel the dull weight of boredom bearing down oppressively. But then the chimes ring again and the announcer declares that the train will be delayed for a whole day. Moreover, having had your ticket checked, you are not allowed to exit the station, while your haul of luggage prohibits you from even leaving your seat. Then you notice that you are all alone in the station, with no one to talk to. Worse still, you have no books or other distractions to alleviate the long hours that lie ahead. Finally, a peculiar medical condition means that you are unable to keep your eyes open for any length of time, so you can't even play I-spy with yourself. In such circumstances, you might imagine that you would plummet to the deepest depths of boredom.

And yet some people deliberately try to cultivate just this sort of situation – a prolonged abstension from distraction or stimulation – in order to meditate. Indeed, although this chapter isn't about meditation, it was a provocative question about the practice that set me wondering about the potential value of boredom. I came across it in Robert M. Pirsig's classic *Zen and the Art of Motorcycle Maintenance*, which I alluded to in the chapter on sadness. As you will recall, Pirsig and his young son are travelling across the great central plains of North America – depicted as a stark, featureless landscape of almost suffocating monotony. He muses that locals who have grown accustomed to this kind of existential quietude might be able to notice subtle moments of beauty that people who are caught up in the sensory overload of the city would probably overlook: a tiny flower poking out of the dirt; a soft, fragrant breeze; a gentle ripple in the cloudscape. Such fleeting graces might be spotted, Pirsig suggests, only 'because other things are absent'.[1] This observation prompts him to reflect on the curious Zen meditation practice of 'just sitting'. The label is apt: the meditator does indeed 'just sit' in order to notice the sights and sounds that float through his or her consciousness. Pirsig writes, 'Zen has something to say about boredom. Its main practice of "just sitting" has got to be the world's most boring activity ... You don't do anything much; not move, not think, not care. What could be more boring? Yet in the very center of this boredom is the very thing Zen Buddhism seeks to teach. What is it? What is it at the very center of boredom that you're not seeing?'[2]

What indeed? As a rich tradition of spiritual literature has intimated – and as a wealth of scientific research has corroborated – meditation can be a portal to some of the most extraordinary, transcendent states of mind that human beings are capable of encountering. And these liberating, life-changing experiences can be found at the very heart of boredom.

Re-envisioning Boredom

Boredom has traditionally had a bad reputation. That said, the word itself is relatively new. It entered the English language in 1852, when Charles Dickens creatively adapted the verb 'to bore' – meaning to pierce or wear down – in order to convey the full extent of Lady Dedlock's desolate mental state in *Bleak House*, in which she is repeatedly described as being 'bored to death' with her life.[3] While 'boredom' is a modern word, though, the state of malaise it describes – a dispiriting combination of frustration, surfeit, sadness, disgust, indifference, apathy and confinement – has been recognised throughout history. One of the earliest surviving literary works is the Sumerian *Epic of Gilgamesh*. It begins with the Mesopotamian King Uruk 'oppressed by idleness'. This state of ennui then becomes the premise for the rest of the story, since it prompts Uruk to embark on a quest to discover a sense of purpose and build a legacy worthy of his name. A little later, in classical Greek and Roman philosophy, comparable states to boredom take on weighty existential overtones that verge on despair. For instance, the Stoic philosopher Seneca, who lived at the same time as Jesus, laments the ubiquity of *taedium vitae* – or 'tiredness of life' – which he describes chillingly as 'the tumult of a soul fixated on nothing'.[4]

By medieval times, boredom had assumed shades of spiritual listlessness and melancholia in the form of *acedia*. Christians would refer to the 'demon of noontide', while Thomas Aquinas called *acedia* the 'sorrow of the world' and the 'enemy of spiritual joy'. Then, as Christianity started to lose its grip on the Western world, this melancholia was reconfigured as the more existential state of *anomie*. This was evident in the so-called 'English disease' of the eighteenth century, the *mal de siècle* of nineteenth-century Europe, and the 'nausea' that continental philosophers bemoaned in the early years of the twentieth century. Finally, modern medicine and psychiatry have essentially taken these varied states – from *taedium vitae* to *acedia* – and re-conceptualised them under the umbrella term *'depression'*.[5] *Meanwhile, 'boredom' itself is simply used to describe dullness or uninterest – a* 'deficit in the quality of life', as Orrin Klapp puts it.[6]

Yet, Pirsig's question – 'What is it at the very center of boredom that you're not seeing?' – gives us pause for thought. When does boredom arise? Most of us would say that it's a negative feeling that occurs when we decide that our current situation lacks value or interest. Ordinarily, as soon as this sensation descends, we start to search for fresh activities or new environs that may hold more promise. But what if we were to stay with the boredom, dive down into it? Then phenomena that appeared to be dull, prosaic or shallow can suddenly become deep wells of mystery and intrigue. In meditation, for example, simply focusing on one's breathing – an activity that we usually take for granted, and one that is rarely regarded as fascinating – can be transformative. This apparently trivial physiological process can teach us invaluable lessons about the nature of the self and usher us into new ways of being. We may realise that our prior assessment of boredom was a product of a limited mindset, not an accurate depiction of our actual situation. Staying with boredom can break down mental barriers and free us from preconceptions that tether us to the mundane. Indeed, we could say that it is a secret gateway to a magical garden of surprise and mystery.

The Magical Garden

'*Alice* was *beginning* to get very tired of sitting by her sister on the bank, and of having nothing to do'.[7] So begins one of the most imaginative adventures in literature. Lewis Carroll dreamed up his immortal tale on the river that wends its way languidly through the otherworldly city of Oxford. One June day in 1862 he was drifting downstream, having set out in a small wooden rowing boat from the perfectly named 'Folly Bridge'. The official weather report recorded the day as cool and rainy, yet he would remember it, appropriately enough, as a 'golden afternoon'. Accompanying Carroll was the Reverend Robinson Duckworth and the three young daughters of Henry Liddell, the Vice Chancellor of Oxford University: Edith, Lorina and ten-year-old Alice. It was a slow, lazy day, and as the party gently meandered along the river, Carroll began to spin his peculiar yarn.

The fictional Alice wonders idly whether the pleasure to be gained from making a daisy chain will be worth the effort of stirring from her slumbers. Then, suddenly, a white rabbit darts by. Nothing unusual in that, but then Alice notices that the rabbit is wearing a waistcoat. Next it draws a watch from one of the pockets and anxiously checks the time. Mightily intrigued, Alice rushes towards the rabbit just in time to see it disappear into a small hole under the hedge. She follows . . . down and down through the darkness, into

Wonderland, a mysterious place of improbable animals and topsy-turvy logic. And all of this begins in a moment of listless boredom.

A similar situation may result in the appearance of our own white rabbit ... if we let it. Usually, when boredom descends, we will do almost anything to distract ourselves, frantically knotting our own daisy-chains, creating the illusion of busy-ness. Should a white rabbit scamper by, we are likely to be too wrapped up in our boredom-busting activities even to notice it. But if we can manage to stay with the boredom, we may be guided down the rabbit hole and enter our own magical realm. I picture this as a verdant garden, full of intriguing features, each of which metaphorically signifies an aspect of the hidden value of boredom.

Taking our first tentative steps into the garden, we encounter a gentle *Stream of Freedom*. We are borne along by the current and come to appreciate the paradoxical idea that having our choices constrained in some way – a restriction that is often characterised as 'boring' – can be liberating. Freed from the burden of constant decision-making, our minds can take flight into higher spheres. The next alluring feature is a beautiful *Polished Stone*. This captures the notion that the monotony of repetition may be necessary for the attainment of perfection, and might even generate valued experiences of absorption in itself. Then we come across a concealed *Diamond Mine*. This embodies the possibility that if we are tethered to a situation that we find dull, by probing deeper we may discover gems just beneath the surface.

Journeying onwards, our new-found perceptual sensitivity reveals a concealed *Well of Creativity*. Drawing deep from this subterranean resource, we are able to tap into the rivers of insight that are hidden within ourselves. Later, we look through the mysterious *Window onto Eternity*, which captures the transcendent idea, articulated by Nobel laureate Joseph Brodsky, that boredom allows us to glimpse the timelessness of the cosmos. Finally, the path leads us to the *Mirror of Clarity*. Here we realise that, in boredom, we may encounter the biggest mystery of all: ourselves. Indeed, it is the fact that we are obliged to confront ourselves that makes boredom so unsettling, but also so powerful and potentially transformative. This is what lies at the heart of boredom, and it is why spiritual traditions like Zen Buddhism prize it so highly.

With that in mind, it's time to go down the rabbit hole.

The Stream of Freedom

You enter a supermarket, looking for some jam. You reach the correct aisle to be greeted by dozens of different brands, all packed tightly on the shelves. Moreover, each brand boasts a variety of flavours, low-sugar options, seedless or seeded, all geared to suit every possible taste and need. Surely this bountiful choice represents the very apex of consumer satisfaction, empowering us to find the jam that is *exactly right*.

Yet Sheena Iyengar and Mark Lepper found out that this almost infinite variety is not the boon we commonly assume it to be.[8] One Saturday, they set up a tasting booth in a grocery store in California and offered passers-by an array of tasty jams. For an hour, their stock consisted of a limited selection of just six different flavours. But then they would reach under the counter and add another twenty-four jars, making a dizzying total of thirty jams. They would offer this wide selection for an hour, then return to the original six options, and so on throughout the day. Contrary to what free-market evangelists would have you believe, shoppers were far more likely to approach the stall when just half a dozen jams were on offer. Moreover, of those who bought some jam, the customers who picked a jar from the six-option display tended to be much happier with their purchase than those who selected from the wider range.

Few concepts animate the Western mind as much as freedom and choice. This is especially true today, as these are the ideological underpinnings of the entire edifice of consumer capitalism. Indeed, surely no one would dare argue that a total absence of freedom is ever desirable. We have witnessed enough horrors – such as slavery – to understand that self-determination is a fundamental human need. Yet, too much freedom – a life unrestricted by any limitations – can be disquieting. The renowned political theorist Cass Sunstein makes this point when writing of the value of 'choosing not to choose'.[9] Take the contrasting situations facing young people at the start of the twentieth century and today. A hundred years ago, their future would have been mapped out. They would usually follow their parents into the family profession, remain in the town where they were born, and marry someone they met at school. Now, someone in their early twenties can aim for pretty much any career, settle almost anywhere in the world, and find the love of their life on the other side of the planet. Such freedom is wonderful, but it can also be a burden. For instance, Søren Kierkegaard argued that unlimited possibility, 'the dizziness of freedom', can be troubling because we must continually make choices that irrevocably determine our fate *and* assume responsibility for the consequences.[10] It was for this reason that Jean-Paul Sartre famously said that we are 'condemned to be free'.[11]

Therefore, the benefits of restricting choice have been recognised. Indeed, some have gone so far as to suggest that this may even be liberating. If you drift downstream, you do not decide where to go. The current simply carries you wherever it will. But this gives you the freedom – and the time – to gaze around, daydream, dwell on deeper concerns. This phenomenon is most evident in monasteries. The monks live within the strictures of highly rigid routines that govern the food they eat, the clothes they wear, and what they may or must do at any given time. Why do they agree to this? In most other settings, such inflexible uniformity would be regarded as supremely boring. And perhaps, on one level, it is for the monks. But it also allows them to free their minds from the whirlpool of inconsequential yet incessant choices that otherwise come to dominate daily existence. ('Should I eat now or in ten minutes' time? Pizza? Unhealthy. Tofu? Disgusting. Pizza then.') The monks are able to dwell on more elevated questions and cultivate a deeper connection to the divine. Indeed, when asked if he could pick just one word to describe the 'secret of happiness', the Dalai Lama replied: 'routines'. Moreover, this kind of 'liberation through restriction' is not only the province of cloistered monks, sequestered away from the world. It can be of value to us all, including some of the most successful people on Earth. Both Barack Obama and Mark Zuckerberg, for example, have described the benefits of only ever wearing one kind of outfit. By removing the burden of sartorial choice, they are free to devote their time to weightier matters.

Of course, it is one thing to choose our own restrictions – and opt for a monastic life or nothing but charcoal-grey suits – and something else entirely to find limits imposed upon us. Sadly, many people suffer just such impositions, especially in their working lives, when they are often obliged to march to the beat of someone else's drum. Nevertheless, liberation may be found here, too. For instance, my work as a psychiatric nursing assistant was particularly restrictive. In addition to the tight scheduling of shift work, just about every aspect of my conduct was regulated – where I was allowed to sit, what I could wear, who I could engage in conversation. These limitations were entirely justifiable – they were all geared towards ensuring the safety of both patients and staff – but they left me with barely any scope for personal choice. You may think that following such a strict set of guidelines would be infuriating, and indeed sometimes it was. But it could also be liberating. The restless, nagging voice that was usually weighing up options, making decisions and rationalising choices remained silent when I was on duty because there was nothing to discuss – everything had already been decided for me. Therefore, I often found myself enjoying a free ride through the events of the day, my mind drifting down the *Stream of Freedom*. Naturally, it was wonderful to regain freedom of choice when I strode out into the fresh night air at the end of a shift. But I also valued those peaceful hours in the hospital when my frantic mind could rest.

The Polished Stone

The next feature in our magical garden is a beautiful polished stone. To understand its significance, it is useful to turn our attention to a small town in Pennsylvania and to a weatherman named Phil Connors – the misanthropic character portrayed by Bill Murray in Harold Ramis's classic film *Groundhog Day*. Connors is sent to Punxsutawney to cover the annual Groundhog Festival, during which the furry creature forecasts whether there will be six more weeks of winter. One of life's great cynics, Connors can barely conceal his disdain for the event, the people of the town and indeed life in general. But then the next day he wakes up and it's Groundhog Day all over again. Everything is exactly the same as the day before, as if on repeat.

His confusion is compounded when all the people in the town react in bewilderment when he asks them, with increasing panic, what is going on. They are mystified by the question because they are living the day for the first time. Only Connors has been cursed with the inexplicable repetition. Then, the next day, it's Groundhog Day again. And the next, and the next. Connors's initial shock soon gives way to licentious hedonism when he realises he can do exactly what he wants and get away with it – bank robbery, joy-riding, a series of one-night stands. Each morning, the clock resets and there are no consequences. But then this unbridled self-gratification begins to pall. *Nothing* he does matters. Desperate and despairing, he wants out and decides to kill himself. But after each suicide he simply wakes up again on Groundhog Day.

Movie buffs love this film for its wit and charm, but it has also found favour in somewhat less predictable quarters. For instance, Catholics have interpreted Connors's time-loop as a depiction of purgatory – the state that sinners must endure until they attain the necessary 'purification' to enter heaven. Somewhat similarly, Buddhists have seen it as an allegory of the endless cycle of birth, death and rebirth in which we are all trapped until we are able to attain enlightenment. Less metaphysically, psychologists have suggested that *Groundhog Day* teaches us that our lives will be unhappy unless and until we begin to work on ourselves and strive to be better people – not for the rewards or status that such progress may bring, but for its own sake. Connors eventually works out that he might as well put the time he has been given to good use. So he learns the piano, becomes an expert ice-sculptor, and even saves a number of lives. Unbeknown to him, these acts of personal development and kindness will eventually allow him to escape from purgatory, but the key point is that he does them every day. Working on ourselves, improving ourselves, demands *repetition*. We don't become better people through half-hearted, one-off actions. Personal growth requires the patient accumulation of continual effort, just as the stone in our garden achieved its beautiful sheen only through regular, meticulous polishing.

You may think that such repetitive activity will be hugely boring. And indeed it can be, at least at first. For instance, as anyone who has ever tried to learn a musical instrument will tell you, practising scales every day is mind-numbing. As soon as I picked up a guitar as a teenager, all I wanted was for my fingers to move like greased lightning over the fretboard like Hendrix's. Yet I knew that I had to plod along monotonously for months, fumbling over my arpeggios, because we can only ever reach excellence through this kind of repetition (not that I ever quite made it). Malcolm Gladwell has popularised this notion through his '10,000-hour rule',[12] which draws on research by Anders Ericsson and colleagues.[13] The Beatles played and practised for over 1200 gigs in Hamburg between 1960 and

1964, which allowed them to accumulate over 10,000 hours of playing time. Thanks to his fortuitous access to a computer in high school, Bill Gates had amassed at least 10,000 hours of programming experience by early adulthood. Gladwell himself totted up the requisite hours of writing during his decade in journalism. OK, the precise figure of 10,000 – roughly twenty hours a week for ten years – may be somewhat arbitrary, but Gladwell's basic message is irrefutable: to achieve excellence in any field, beyond any raw talent we might possess, we need to knuckle down and practise for a significant period of time. You might even argue that the excellence is the reward for enduring the boredom of the repetition.

This is not the end of the story, though, because there is even a chance that the repetition may cease to be boring. Indeed, it can become an art in itself, or even, as Mihaly Csikszentmihalyi suggested, one of the highlights of life.[14] Csikszentmihalyi set out to discover which activities people found most rewarding. He gave each of the participants in his study a pager (the experiment began in the 1980s), and over subsequent weeks and months sent them intermittent messages. Upon this cue, the participants had to note down what they were doing at that precise moment, and rate it in terms of enjoyment on a scale of one to ten. Csikszentmihalyi found that the participants most enjoyed any activity that demanded skill and in which the difficulty of the task perfectly matched their ability to execute it well. These activities ranged wildly – from a pianist mastering a sonata to a rock-climber tackling a fiendishly difficult route – but each and every participant reported feeling absorbed in their repetitive practice. The intensity of their concentration was such that they lost all track of time, forgot their usual preoccupations, and became utterly immersed in what they were doing. Csikszentmihalyi labelled this captivating state of consciousness – which is similar to the peak experiences discussed in the previous chapter – 'flow'.

Anyone who devotes considerable time and effort to a particular skill, whether at work or as a hobby, will be familiar with this state of being. Perhaps you enjoy running or swimming, two activities that are the very definition of repetitive, since one employs the same muscle movements again and again. Both sports can feel boring, at least initially. For instance, I swim regularly, and during the first few lengths my mind usually complains about the dullness of ploughing up and down the lane. The clock on the wall seems to slow to a crawl, with the hour I have allocated to my pool session stretching out like a grey, characterless mass. I often wonder how I'll last even ten minutes. But then I usually cross the threshold of boredom, the rhythmic movements lead me into 'the zone' and I become one with the action. The repetition, which had seemed so boring at first, becomes transformative. I am no longer an individual who is undertaking an activity, but a flowing together of person, place and task in one seamless process.

So, through repetition, we not only polish the stone of our character to a glittering sheen, but may come to value the act of polishing itself. Similar revelations can also be found in our next source of wonder: the *Diamond Mine*.

The Diamond Mine

The experimental musician John Cage once said, 'If something is boring after two minutes, try it for four. If still boring, then eight. Then sixteen. Then thirty-two. Eventually one discovers that it is not boring at all'.[15] This is a perfect illustration of the idea that is central to this chapter: nothing is *intrinsically* boring. Boredom arises only because of our preconceptions, because we have prejudged something to be boring. But our judgement can change. And if it does, it's like finding a *Diamond Mine* at the side of a dirt track. There are concealed gems there – precious stones that we never expected to find.

Picture yourself setting off on a long-awaited holiday to a favourite resort. You wend your way through a series of towns and villages that you barely notice, such is your desire to reach your destination. If you were to hazard a guess, you'd say that all of these places are pretty boring. Then, as you enter a particularly nondescript village, your car judders to a halt. You have a look under the bonnet and realise that you won't be going any further until the local garage opens. Moreover, it's a late Friday afternoon in the middle of the summer holidays, so that won't be for at least three days. You're stuck. Your grand holiday plans have gone up in smoke.

At first, it seems like a catastrophe. You need a drink, so you head to the local pub. A group of old men are sitting in the corner, nursing their pints, which hardly mitigates your concern about how dull the weekend will be. But then you have another look at them. Given their ages, they are probably war veterans, surviving the war's horrors through a combination of inconceivable courage and good fortune. They lived through the Swinging Sixties, the Cold War and the Space Race. You start to imagine the stories they could tell, then realise that you don't have to imagine them. You walk over to their table, explain your predicament and they invite you to join them. Three hours later, you leave the pub having heard a compendium of tales of daring and adventure, ecstasy and heartbreak, fact and (probably) a fair amount of fiction. These men are diamonds.

There is nothing unusual about this scenario – almost anything can become interesting, if we let it. The human mind is like a motion-activated camera that operates on a hair-trigger, darting around to capture any sudden movement.[16] Scratch your arm and – *swoosh* – your attention is immediately drawn to the spot. Hear a loud sound outside and – *swoosh* – your focus swivels to the window. Your pet dog jumps up on the table and – *swoosh* – your eyes flash over to the disobedient mutt. Our attention is drawn to stimuli that our brain, generally without much conscious thought, has decided are novel or salient – things we feel we need to check out urgently. This reflexive and intuitive mechanism has served us very well throughout our evolutionary history, keeping us alert to the dangers of the snake that suddenly rears out of the bushes or the crumbling path on the cliff edge. Unfortunately, though, it means that we tend to categorise familiar phenomena as boring. They certainly don't get the heart pumping and grab our attention in the same way as flashing lights and loud noises do. And yet, if you force yourself to focus on these 'duller' phenomena, your mind will discover the gems that lie beneath the surface, and come to appreciate their significance and meaning. You just need to stop it swivelling around like an adrenaline junkie in search of the next fix.

Here, it's useful to return to the idea of meditation. This isn't a cue for non-Buddhists to skip to the next page, because we all meditate every day. In essence, the practice involves nothing more than focusing on something in a curious, caring and interested way. So, a fisherman watching his line for a nibble is meditating, as is a mother who gazes at her baby's face, waiting for a smile. In formal meditation practice, the only difference is that practitioners harness this natural attentiveness and direct it towards phenomena that we would usually disregard. For instance, one common technique is the 'mindfulness of breathing'. Here, meditators figuratively 'watch' their breath, registering the act of breathing itself – sometimes by counting each inhalation and exhalation – and trying to be sensitive to how the process feels. One of the technique's most immediate benefits is that it can be very calming – not for nothing are we told to count to ten when we feel angry – but it can be much more interesting than that. Indeed, the attentiveness *makes* the practice itself interesting.

Meditators report that the breath can become a source of great fascination, and they start to detect subtle depths and nuances that they never suspected were there. It may even lead to profound personal insights. It is common, for instance, for practitioners to realise that the 'self' – who we are, deep down – is not a fixed, static, internal object. Rather, as the meditator perceives the intricate dynamics of respiration, they start to understand that the self is a similarly fluid process, a confluence of ever-changing streams of internal phenomena – from the gentle undulations of breathing, to the rivers of thought in the mind's consciousness. But whatever insights may arise, and however we meditate – be it in a temple or on a river bank – focusing our attention can reveal value and interest in even the most apparently prosaic phenomena. Furthermore, viewing the world in this way leads directly to the next magical feature in the garden: the *Well of Creativity*.

The Well of Creativity

In 1410, work began on a series of twelve large statues of Old Testament characters to grace the Duomo in Florence. Half a century later, Agostino di Duccio was entrusted with the task of sculpting David, Israel's second king and the slayer of Goliath. He set to work on an immense six-metre-high slab of marble, hewn out of a quarry in northern Tuscany. But two years later, for reasons that remain unclear, he downed tools, leaving a rough, ill-shaped hulk of stone. The marble ghoul lay untouched for the next thirty-five years, haunting the cathedral's workshop, much to the chagrin of the authorities. In 1500, they decided something must be done and began the search for someone who might finish the job. They considered the eminent Leonardo da Vinci, but finally handed the commission to a young talent of rare genius, Michelangelo, who was just twenty-six at the time. According to legend, at first he just sat and stared at the giant slab of marble for days on end. Asked why he wasn't getting on with the task and busily attacking the stone with his chisel, he retorted: '*Sto lavorando!*' (I'm working). His reflective vigil lasted almost a month, until, on the 13 September 1501, he finally started carving. When his masterpiece was unveiled more than two years later, he was asked how he had created a work of such transcendent beauty. He replied, 'I saw an angel in the marble and carved until I set him free.'

Michelangelo is a perfect illustration of the idea that creativity requires the time and space afforded by inaction in order to flourish. I'm not suggesting that he was bored during that month of sitting and staring (although he may have been at times), but he certainly understood that stillness and silence often lead to inspiration. Boredom provides the clearing space for just this kind of quiet reflection, albeit in an enforced and unchosen way. So, what if we were to view boredom as the arena in which our own Michelangelo might awaken? Might we also see angels and set them free?

Inactivity is so germane to creativity because busyness is the enemy of insight and illumination. Rushing headlong into tasks leaves no time for our bashful muse to emerge from the shadows. Instead, we should sit and linger, as a fisherman waits patiently for a bite, and allow the lightning flash of inspiration to arrive. We see this process at work in countless examples of creative genius. For instance, the young Albert Einstein spent nearly seven years as a lowly patent clerk while he finished his thesis and searched for an academic position. Although the job could be extremely repetitive, this dullness gave his mind a chance to wander. The Special Theory of Relativity came to him while he daydreamed of riding a sunbeam to the edge of the universe. Indeed, it was in the middle of his stint in the patent office, in 1905, when he had his *annus mirabilis*, during which he wrote four papers that would revolutionise physics and transform our understanding of the cosmos. Similarly, René Descartes was said to have conceived the mathematical concept of x and y – the basis of every graph – while staring absently at a fly tottering around the corner of a room.

As these two scientific titans illustrate, the languid spaciousness of boredom and inactivity may allow us to forge new and unexpected connections. Most acts of creativity don't involve someone summoning new ideas out of nowhere. Novelists rarely invent new words to get their stories across, and composers would struggle to conjure up new notes for their symphonies. Rather, their skill lies in stringing together existing words in innovative ways, and fashioning new melodies out of the standard twelve-note scale. But these moments of inspiration cannot be willed or forced into being simply by concentrating the rational mind; if they could, we would all be able to turn on creativity like a tap. Instead, the conscious mind must pause, cease whirring, which allows the *subconscious* mind to establish new links as bubbles of inspiration rise from the depths. This pause may seem like inaction, and may even feel rather boring. Hence, the rational mind usually tries to kick back into gear and find new distractions. But if we force ourselves to linger within the boredom, magical things will start to unfold beneath the surface. As Friedrich Nietzsche wrote, 'For thinkers and all sensitive spirits, boredom is that disagreeable "windless calm" of the soul that precedes a happy voyage and cheerful winds. They have to bear it and must wait for its effect on them.'[17]

Strikingly, neuroscience is starting to corroborate such poetic assessments of the subtle virtues of boredom. This cutting-edge field of research allows us to peer into our inner space and probe the previously hidden secrets of the brain. We can see, in real time, the pulsing activity of this mysterious three-pound organ – by far the most complex and bewildering object in the known universe, the source and substance of all that we experience and all that we are. Until fairly recently, the consensus was that the brain effectively winds down whenever we are not engaged in a specific mental task. But then, in 2001, Marcus Raichle noticed an unusual pattern of brain activity that quietly clicks into gear every time we are *not* focused on a task. He labelled the intricate circuit of interconnected brain regions where this occurs the Default Mode Network (DMN).[18] Ever since, neuroscientists have explored this mysterious DMN, and they are now linking it to artistic creativity,[19] the creation of thoughts,[20] our sense of self,[21] even consciousness itself.[22] And boredom seems to play a crucial role in awakening the DMN, allowing it to spark into life.[23] When that happens, our brains are free to wander into unfamiliar, mist-shrouded valleys of uncreated thought, where we may chance upon unexpected discoveries and forge new connections – the very essence of creativity and innovation.

Boredom may even generate insights into the nature of time itself by unveiling the *Window onto Eternity*.

The Window onto Eternity

In *Catch-22*, Joseph Heller's biting satire on the insanity of war, the airman Dunbar's principal ambition is to make his life last as long as possible. He figures that the best way to achieve this – apart from avoiding getting shot down – is to cultivate boredom. So, we learn that he loved skeet-shooting because 'he hated every minute of it'.[24] Hence, time stretched out interminably.

After explaining his reasoning to his sceptical comrades, one of them argues, 'Maybe a long life does have to be filled with many unpleasant conditions if it's to seem long. But in that event, who wants one?'

'I do,' Dunbar replies.

'Why?' asks his colleague.

'What else is there?'[25]

What else indeed? Perhaps Dunbar is right: immersing oneself in boredom is a sure-fire way to lengthen one's days. That said, as we've seen above, boredom is not necessarily unpleasant. If we engage with it in the right spirit, it can even be a source of wonder and inspiration. But whatever shade boredom may take, when we experience it time always seems to slow, stretching out inexorably into the far distance. Studies of time perception confirm what we already know from personal experience: when we are bored, the hands of the clock really do appear to grind almost to a standstill, with the minutes and hours passing as if in slow motion.[26] Whereas in moments of exhilaration and merriment time slips through our fingers like grains of sand, in boredom it is sluggish and heavy, dragging on and on.

During my first summer of university, I embarked on an expedition to Tibet with a few friends. The trip was mind-blowing, exploding my narrow horizons. And yet, despite all the intense, Technicolor images that come to mind when I think of those months away – from eating yak butter on a mountain peak, to teaching Beatles songs to a group of giggling teenage monks in Lhasa – one of my strongest memories is of an experience of profound boredom. While my friends continued on to Nepal, I travelled alone over to the east coast of China to take up a summer job in Qingdao, where I had taught English the previous year. I made the ridiculous decision to do the journey – traversing the whole of that vast country – in one fell swoop, which meant remaining on a train for four days in a row. Moreover, I was trying to watch my pennies, so I opted for a painful, hard-backed seat, rather than forking out a little extra for a sleeper berth, so I barely slept at all. As bad as the length and discomfort of the journey were, though, the main issue was I had *nothing* to do. My companions had gone in the other direction, and I had no books, no music, no idea.

With no distractions, those four days stretched into an eternity. Trapped within the stultifying metal carriage, which creaked for mile after mile through monotonous landscapes, I had no means of 'passing the time'. Everything slowed to a lazy crawl, clock hands almost motionless, hours stretching into days. There were even moments when the train and all of the passengers, including me, seemed to stop altogether, marooned in suspended animation. Above all, I started to *feel* time as a physical presence. It became solid, thick, gelatinous, oozing over everything – like the melting clocks in a Dalí painting. Indeed, Martin Heidegger wrote that boredom is the physical experience of time, and of our existence through time.[27] Rather than seeing it as a 'mood', he suggested that it is an 'existential orientation' during which we come face to face with the nature of time itself. In a similar vein, Joseph Brodsky argued that boredom 'represents pure, undiluted time in all its repetitive, redundant, monotonous splendor'.[28]

So, boredom allows us to experience the visceral reality of time, but does that mean we should *value* it? Both Heidegger and Brodsky insisted that we should, although for different reasons. Brodsky argued that boredom is our 'window on time's infinity', which can lead us to reassess our place in the cosmos by allowing us to see our lives from the 'perspective of eternity'. From this elevated standpoint, we are able to relativise all of our daily worries and concerns and minimise them to the point of meaninglessness. We see that our life is just a tiny, ephemeral spark in the vast, eternal furnace of the universe, so fleeting and minuscule as barely to register. This can be a sobering and even troubling notion, and may prompt the question: 'Does anything I do really matter?' Alternatively, it can be enormously liberating. If *I* don't matter, given the incomprehensibly vast nature of the cosmos, then surely those problems that are troubling me are even less important.

Heidegger approached the issue from a rather different angle. He argued that the glimpse of time's eternity – which we experience most often when we are bored – can be a powerful call to arms. Hence, he urged us to use boredom to 'wake up', not because it reveals that our actions don't matter, but because it proves that they *do*. His principal message, gleaned from the perspective of eternity, and from the realisation that our existence is all too brief, is *carpe diem*: seize the day, make every moment count.

Either way, whether we agree with Brodsky or Heidegger, the glimpse of eternity that boredom affords certainly provides a transformative lesson about existence. Equally, boredom can also let us see *ourselves* clearly, which brings us to the final object in the garden: the *Mirror of Clarity*.

The Mirror of Clarity

Back in the fifth century AD, there was a prince in southern India named Bodhidharma. Although he was a favoured son of the king, he did not crave political power or prestige. Instead, he sought a life of contemplation and became a Buddhist monk. His master saw Bodhidharma's potential and chose him to export Buddhism to China, so he crossed the border and wandered into the warm southern provinces. His public displays of meditation swiftly earned him renown, as well as an audience with the Emperor Wu. But when Bodhidharma refused to give Wu the recognition he felt he deserved, the emperor promptly banished him. Bodhidharma ventured into the cold northern regions and eventually found shelter in a mountainside cave, high above a Shaolin temple. According to legend, he spent the next nine years meditating in the dark, facing the inner wall of the cavern. Such was his subsequent influence that Zen masters would attempt to emulate him by meditating in front of a bare wall.

At the start of this chapter, we contemplated sitting in an empty station for a whole day with no distractions. What about sitting alone in a cave for nine years? What on earth did Bodhidharma do for almost a decade? More importantly, why did he choose to remain there?

This brings me back to my seemingly endless journey across China. Beyond the uncanny feeling that I was immersed in the thick treacle of time, I also experienced the vertiginous sensation of encountering myself. Such encounters are increasingly rare these days. Our waking lives have been colonised by numerous gadgets that are all designed to ensure we never get bored. Every commuter will be familiar with the scene of dozens of faces hypnotised by the faint glow of smartphones, all of them totally disconnected from their surroundings. I'm as guilty of this as anyone else. On the train into work, I check my emails, browse through the news, and perhaps find nothing of interest. At that point, I put the phone back in my pocket, but a few minutes – or even seconds – later, as if scratching an existential itch, I'll get the phone out again and perform the self-same searches. What am I expecting to find? Or – perhaps more pertinently – what am I trying to avoid?

On that interminable train ride through China, the bore-dom troubled me at first. I experienced agitation, even mild panic. But eventually I accepted that I would just have to sit and *be* with myself. Perhaps this is what we are trying to side-step when we seek refuge in our phones. Indeed, it may be that many of our activities are undertaken precisely to avoid encountering ourselves. But why are we so afraid? What happens when we come face to face with ourselves in the *Mirror of Clarity*?

In my experience, during those hundred hours on a Chinese train, in addition to making my way to Qingdao I went on a journey of self-revelation. I found that the boredom gradu-ally created an empty space into which unfamiliar thoughts and sensations could enter freely. Removed from the frantic busyness of humdrum distractions, and from the attendant whirlpools of mundane thoughts – what to eat, wear, say, do – I began to discover the quiet depths of the mind that are usually concealed. I encountered hidden dimensions of myself, thoughts and feelings I had not realised I harboured. I toured through long-dormant memories, presented in a slide-show of fragments from the past. I even gained new perspectives on long-gestating problems, and began to craft potential solutions. Not all of these self-revelations were pleasant, and the relief was blissful when the train finally arrived at Qingdao, but they were invariably useful, valuable, even precious. They did not comprise a complete, Socratic, 'know thyself' form of self-awareness, but over those four days I did get to know myself a little better.

Since then, I have learned to appreciate boredom as a chance to voyage into uncharted inner territory . . . at least to some extent. I'm still human – I don't *seek out* boredom – but if I find myself in a situation that feels boring, I try to resist fleeing into distraction immediately, and instead endeavour just to *be* for a while. True, the dullness may persist, but often I start to experience revealing self-observations. Over time, especially when these observations recur, I begin to recognise habitual patterns of thinking, the tracks on which my trains of thought tend to run. For instance, whenever I leave the house, my mind tends to turn itself in knots – I worry that I've left the door unlocked or the gas ring on. Then, later in the day, during a period of boredom, I'll watch those anxious thoughts swimming around my mind, like agitated fish. As I continue to observe, though, the thoughts gradually become less frenzied as I start to understand them, or even befriend them. This has taught me that I don't necessarily need to heed their warnings: they are just records that my mind plays automatically, not alarms that demand immediate action. Conversely, I've also encountered thoughts that I never knew I had inside me – perhaps flashes of inspiration from the *Well of Creativity*. Such insights can certainly arrive during moments of busyness and activity – walking is particularly effective for this – but they seem to emerge more often when I'm bored.

Needless to say, there's no need to sit in a cave and stare at a wall for nine years to get to know ourselves in this way. We don't even need to meditate … or at least it's not necessary to sit cross-legged on a cushion in a temple. We just need to be present to ourselves, without distractions, for a few minutes. Then it may be an idea to build up to a longer journey, which might generate deeper revelations. As Osho said, when reflecting on Zen 'wall-sitting' meditation, 'Watching the wall – slowly, slowly thoughts disappear, thinking stops, mind evaporates and what is left is your authentic reality'.[29] But if this kind of intensive meditation is a step too far, we can still catch brief glimpses of ourselves in the mirror. For instance, on the weary commute home, refrain from checking your phone for the fifth time and allow yourself simply to *be*. This may reveal anything from the valuable jewels of the *Diamond Mind* and the inspiration of the *Well of Creativity*, to the existential insights that lie through the *Window onto Eternity* and the understanding that we see in the *Mirror of Clarity*.

This journey towards self-revelation can go very deep indeed, but it is not only occasioned by boredom. Arguably, we may venture even deeper into ourselves when we arrive in the remote territory of loneliness, as our penultimate chapter explores.

CHAPTER SEVEN

Loneliness

It could be said that we are more connected than ever. Advances in technology, especially the Internet and the mobile phone, mean that a world of people is now just a click or a call away. But it doesn't necessarily follow that we feel bonded, supported, nurtured. Indeed, just as these globalising technologies are bringing people together, they are flinging us apart. Gone are the days when most of us grew up and grew old in one place, surrounded by a reliable network of family and friends. Now we migrate from city to city, or even country to country, in search of work, love, safety or adventure; and there is an increasing tendency to keep on moving, with the result that we never feel truly settled. Families and friendship networks become scattered and stretched, held together by no more than the ephemeral strands of the World Wide Web. Moreover, although we *can* connect to our loved ones via the modern miracles of technology, many of our hours are still spent in lonely isolation as we commute, eat, work or live alone. Millions of us lead atomised, individual lives, even – or perhaps especially – if we live in crowded urban conurbations. As a result, loneliness has become one of the banes of the twenty-first century.

And yet, while all of us would say that we hate to feel lonely, we would also admit that we sometimes long to be alone. The extent and shape of this need for isolation can vary widely, of course. At the farthest extreme, an ascetic like Bodhidharma may wish to spend years alone in a cave. Meanwhile, a gregarious extrovert may require only the occasional minute or two of peace and quiet to regroup and gather his energy. Either way, we all need at least some time and space away from our burdens of social responsibility, from having to present our best face to the crowd. We need those oases of calm when we can retreat into ourselves and find some peace away from the hustle and bustle of conversation, the give and take of interaction. This doesn't necessarily involve withdrawing *physically*. Sometimes, aloneness can be achieved simply by finding the space to be with your thoughts. Indeed, those who care for us can remain close by, present in a loving way, while still granting this type of aloneness. Think of your partner holding you close at the end of a hard day, without asking for explanations or cajoling you to talk through your problems. In such situations we feel both cared for and alone. There is a term for this much-desired form of aloneness: *solitude*.

This differs greatly from loneliness. Solitude is aloneness that is both sought and cherished, while loneliness is aloneness that is resented or feared. As the theologian Paul Tillich said, 'Language has created the word "loneliness" to express the pain of being alone. And it has created the word "solitude" to express the glory of being alone'.[1] Yet, these two states are not worlds apart from each other. Rather, at some point, solitude silently crosses a dark, imperceptible boundary and becomes loneliness. For our ascetic hermit, although the first year away from society might seem like bliss, over the next few months he might start to feel the cold touch of loneliness. On the other hand, the life and soul of the party might crave company after just ten minutes of isolation. Whatever our level of sociability, though, whatever our 'limit', if we exceed it, we suffer the pain of loneliness.

Intriguingly, though, this limit is not set in stone for any of us – it shifts, depending on circumstances. For instance, you might be walking alone through a park and suffer a sudden pang of loneliness. Then, the very next moment, a ray of sunshine might flicker onto your face just as a bird sings and you catch the scent of roses in the air. Suddenly, you may feel altogether more hopeful about life and more at peace as your loneliness transforms into solitude.

Our main task in this chapter is to learn how to do just that: ease the pain of loneliness and turn it into the grace of solitude.

From Loneliness to Solitude

It's a lazy Saturday morning in the suburbs. You wake up in an empty house with the day stretching out before you in dull monochrome. You've made no plans, and no invitations are beckoning. Over breakfast, you wonder how you will fill the day. Sitting at the kitchen table, you suddenly start to feel very lonely. You are physically alone in the house, but your loneliness runs deeper than that. It's as if you are emotionally isolated from the rest of the world, like you've fallen off the radar. You know that your friends and loved ones care for you, but for some reason you feel that you can't reach out to them right now. Your only option seems to be to get out and about, so you decide to take a trip into town. At least there's plenty to do there, and it might feel good to be among the crowds.

You wander down the road to the station and stand uncertainly on the platform with a small scattering of fellow lost souls. You board the train and begin to hurtle towards the city centre. Ever more passengers crowd into the carriage at each stop and the volume rises, a querulous chirruping of at least a dozen different languages. You start to feel claustrophobic as the train fills to overflowing, so you're grateful when you finally reach your destination. After disembarking you breathe the cool air with relief, but on the street the crowds are even more intense – a vast tide of humanity sweeping past you, anonymous face after anonymous face. No one even glances at you: everyone seems to be in a couple or a group, or gazing at their phones, or simply barrelling ahead with grim determination. You feel invisible. You are passing through all of these people's lives unseen. You may as well not exist. If anything, the loneliness is even deeper than before, when you were sitting on your own at home. All of these unregarding faces merely heighten your sense of disconnection. You feel cut adrift in this sea of humanity.

But then the day suddenly takes a turn for the better. A friend phones unexpectedly to invite you out for a drink this evening, or to tell you about the party they're holding next week. Or a stranger on the street looks in your direction and smiles. Or the Christmas decorations in a shop window cause you to think about seeing your mum and dad for the first time in months. Or you pass a travel agency and fantasise about a trip abroad. Or you chance upon a really talented busker, or a Salvation Army choir singing carols, or a previously unexplored modern art gallery. The tide of people suddenly seems gentler, less oppressive. Although you still know none of them, you don't feel so isolated any more as you start to feel the warmth of common humanity. Perhaps you gaze around at the other visitors in that gallery, all of them peering intently at the paintings, trying to work out what they mean. At this point, you may even start to *appreciate* being there on your own. You have the space and the time to let your thoughts emerge, to work out what you feel about the art. You might also congratulate yourself on doing something worthwhile with your day. Even though you're still surrounded by dozens of people you don't know, your sense of loneliness has transformed into solitude: you are now content with your aloneness.

As this scenario reveals, the presence – or absence – of other people has little bearing on either solitude or loneliness. Each of them is a state of mind. If you are happy within yourself in the middle of a crowd, and feel no need to interact with those around you, then that is solitude.

On the train home, you no longer feel lonely or invisible, even though your fellow travellers' reactions towards you are identical to those you experienced this morning. Now you don't mind that no one catches your eye or flashes a smile because your mind is at rest, having found tranquillity in the gallery, or in whatever it was that brightened your day. In fact, you crave even greater solitude, away from all the hubbub. So you're glad when you reach the station, walk home and can be truly alone with your peace.

Turning Loneliness into Solitude

So, loneliness and solitude are merely two contrasting ways of viewing a situation. On the one hand, this means there is a risk of peaceful solitude slipping into the darker realm of loneliness. On the other, though, we have the potential to transform loneliness into solitude. When we feel lonely, we might begin to hear the gentle clamour of urges and inclinations that are often overlooked when we are among company. These aspects of our personality may be reluctant to emerge when we are around other people, but they can prove to be precious assets if they manage to make themselves heard in the space provided by loneliness, guiding us towards well-being. Indeed, we will discover that loneliness starts to turn into solitude at the very moment when these inner elements first raise their voices.

The chapter is populated by six metaphorical figures, with the first somewhat different from the other five. Our main aim, as I've suggested, is to transform the pain of loneliness into the peace of solitude. This involves learning to appreciate the potential value and beauty of aloneness, rather than trying to 'solve' it through a continual search for company. Sometimes, though, it *is* possible to alleviate loneliness simply by reaching out and connecting with other people. With this in mind, the first figure is the *Bond Maker*, who gives us the courage to take a leap of faith, jump outside our comfort zone and forge new bonds with strangers. However, at other times, it is not possible to take this leap, for whatever reason. Thereafter, the remaining five figures help with the greater issue of transforming loneliness into the valuable state of solitude.

The second figure is the *Free Thinker*. Here, our aloneness empowers us to develop independent thought, reducing our tendency to be swayed by the masses and helping us to heed the call of our own authentic reasoning. Similarly, the *Soul Singer* reflects the idea that we are able to truly tune into our deepest feelings – and express them – only when we are alone. Next, the *Fighter* captures the notion that we often find out just how strong and courageous we can be when we are compelled to go into battle alone. In such circumstances, we may discover levels of fortitude and mettle that we never suspected we possessed.

We move into more mystical terrain with our penultimate figure. The *Light Seeker* may lead us into more elevated realms of the soul, but only if we take a step back from the world and relinquish convention. Finally, our spiritual gaze turns outwards when we encounter the dreamy *Star Gazer*, as we develop a deep appreciation and even reverence for the splendours of the natural world.

First, though, before we learn how to transform loneliness into solitude, we should explore the simple expedient of alleviating it by connecting with people.

The Bond Maker

In my twenties, I would often go on holiday alone. For the most part, these were not wild, far-flung expeditions – more a case of a week or two in France, courtesy of a budget airline. Nor were they frantic escape bids. I generally loved my life in Edinburgh, knocking around with the band, enjoying the camaraderie of a group of good friends. The trips were really just brief times out, stepping out of the stream of life for a while. I would often stay in a small caravan in a dusty campsite on the Mediterranean coast. It was remote enough to feel as though I was off the radar, yet still within a lazy stroll of a decent supermarket. While I was there, I invariably found the solitude good for my soul, delivering the precious gifts that aloneness can bring. I was beholden to no one, and could wander where I pleased around the cobblestoned streets of the nearby town. My thoughts had the space to bubble up inside me, and I had the time to shape them into songs that I could present to the band on my return. My inner *Star Gazer* could revel in the quiet delights of the natural world as I sat quietly on the beach and let my heart fill with the gentle lapping of the waves. On the whole, I loved these little trips.

But not always. Even though I sought out and cherished the solitude, at times it would cross the dark line into loneliness. I was generally fine during the daytime, when the Mediterranean light made everything sparkle. But as night fell, my aloneness could become more troublesome, less welcome. If I heard my fellow holidaymakers eating and socialising together, the darkness would start to feel oppressive and I would long for company. So, I would walk down to the beach, where groups of youths would always be huddled around campfires, laughing and drinking, singing Manu Chao or Bob Marley. I longed to join them, but I'm not the type to just walk up to a bunch of strangers and introduce myself. I also couldn't bring myself to slink forlornly away, however, so I'd find some pretext to engage one of them in conversation. Perhaps I'd ask for a bottle opener for my beer, or a light for a cigarette. Sometimes this would lead to a warm welcome, and I might sit with them for an hour or two. At other times, I would feel as if I had overstayed my welcome after just ten minutes. Even that was enough to satisfy my need for human contact, though, and I would leave somewhat replenished, or at least happy that I'd made the effort.

As I mentioned earlier, this chapter is primarily concerned with transforming loneliness into solitude. If you're feeling lonely, it's usually no help to hear, 'Well, go and find some company then,' because it's your very difficulty in doing so that is the root cause of the problem. Urging lonely people to be more sociable is as ineffectual and inappropriate as telling someone who is sad, 'Oh, for goodness' sake, cheer up' (often followed by 'It might never happen'). In certain circumstances, though, we *can* be encouraged to reach out to others and dissolve our loneliness by taking a leap and connecting with strangers. This generally involves stepping out of our comfort zone in some way, adopting an assertiveness or boldness that may be unfamiliar. It's no easy task, of course, but we can harness our loneliness as a motivational, 'bond-making' force that prompts us to take a chance and make that difficult first step. For instance, you might strike up a conversation with someone you've never spoken to before, as I did with the locals on the beach. This is often easier if you push yourself to participate in a structured interaction, like a book group or a dance class, in which the awkwardness of meeting new people is diminished by the fact that you have a shared focus. For those of an older generation, connecting with the grandkids might involve mastering initially unfamiliar gadgets. For those looking for love – and tired of waiting for that spontaneous, star-crossed encounter – it could entail signing up to a dating website.

These latter two examples illustrate the way in which human ingenuity is providing remedies for loneliness. Indeed, we are increasingly adept at harnessing technological innovation to meet our need for interaction ... even if that interaction is not always with other humans. For instance, a Japanese company recently launched a cute, furry robotic seal named Paro. It responds to human warmth and affection in a lifelike way by purring and dreamily closing its eyes, while its electronic brain continually gathers information on these interactions to develop a character profile of its owner and increase its own lovability. Some readers will probably recoil at this channelling of human affection towards an electronic object, but such inventions can be powerful remedies for isolation. In clinical trials, researchers have found that Paro reduces loneliness and increases wellbeing among the elderly and people who are recovering from serious illness.[2] And if it helps – especially in places like Japan, which has an ageing and increasingly lonely population – then why not make full use of it? For some people, it may not be *so* different from other forms of non-human companionship, such as the enduring friendship and affection that a dog or a cat can offer.

Sometimes, then, loneliness can be alleviated. Encouraged by our inner *Bond Maker*, we may feel emboldened to reach out and connect with others. Moreover, experiences of loneliness can increase our appreciation of bond-making, be it with existing connections or with strangers. For instance, during my trips to France, I would realise – half with regret, half with relief – that I was not quite as solitary, independent and self-sufficient as I sometimes thought I was. Countering any romantic notions of being a lone wanderer, I saw clearly how much I needed other people in my life. So, I was grateful for any new acquaintances I might meet while meandering through the streets or strolling down the beach; and even more grateful for the kind, welcoming, loving faces of my family and friends when I returned home. Spending time away from them helped me truly appreciate how much they meant to me.

Sometimes, though, there may be no immediate social 'solution' to loneliness, no easy return into the arms of loved ones. In these cases, as the rest of this chapter explores, our task is to transform loneliness into the more peaceful state of solitude. This involves understanding that certain qualities and strengths of great value have the space to emerge and grow when we are alone. The first of these qualities is the *Free Thinker.*

The Free Thinker

A research team has invited you to participate in an experiment on 'visual judgement'. You sit at a table in a nondescript room with seven other participants. The task you are set seems childishly simple. The researcher holds up a card on which are drawn three straight lines of differing lengths as well as a comparison line. All you are required to do is state which line is the same length as the comparison line. At first glance, the answer seems self-evident: it's line B. You ease back in your seat, ready to state the obvious when your turn comes. The researcher starts with the person who is sitting to your left, then proceeds in a clockwise direction around the table, meaning that you will be the last to answer. One by one, everybody insists that line C is the longest. After the fourth person answers, you have another look at the card.

There is *no way* that C is the correct answer! What is going on? The fifth person answers 'C' and your confusion rises. You even start to experience a sense of panic. You *know* that the others are wrong ... or at least you *think* that they are (doubts are starting to creep in). Of course, the other seven participants are stooges who have been instructed to give the wrong answer. You are the only genuine participant in the room. But you don't know this. So, what do you say when your turn finally comes?

Over recent centuries, writers and philosophers have sounded ominous warnings about the dangers of falling prey to group-think. Martin Heidegger, for instance, felt that much of our existence is structured and determined by what he chillingly called *das Man* – 'the They'.[3] He did not deploy this term in an entirely derogatory way: he acknowledged that we are social creatures, so our common ideas and values – our shared 'horizon' – are essential aspects of what makes us human. But he did argue that the tendency to 'fall' into this mode of existence can be problematic, as it means we are less likely to make our own choices and take responsibility for our own decisions. In the chapter on guilt we saw the danger of ceding decision-making to dominant others, as revealed most starkly by Stanley Milgram in his electric-shock experiment. Similarly, our tendency to acquiesce to the will of *das Man* – even when we know it is wrong – was highlighted in the line-judgement experiment described above, which was devised by Solomon Asch, another great post-war psychologist, in 1951.[4] Whereas Milgram explored the potentially devastating consequences of *obedience*, Asch focused on the equally problematic phenomenon of *conformity*. Strikingly, he found that around 70 per cent of participants went along with the majority opinion. Sometimes the group consensus made the genuine volunteer second-guess and doubt their own perception, and occasionally their sanity. At other times they conformed because they feared the social penalties that might arise from not doing so – such as suffering ridicule or even ostracism. Either way, Heidegger would have accused these conformist participants of behaving 'inauthentically'.

In light of Asch's results – and Heidegger's concerns – the first key benefit of being alone is that we are less likely to follow the crowd. Away from the clamour of others' opinions, demands and judgements, we can hear our own inner voice and follow our own path. To use that compelling modern phrase, we have the freedom to live more *authentically*. This powerful idea of authenticity has a long, distinguished history. Jean-Jacques Rousseau, the eighteenth-century French philosopher, is often credited with introducing the notion to a nation, and indeed a continent, that was thirsty for new modes of self-understanding. Prior to his *Confessions*,[5] only religious figures, such as St Augustine, had ever thought to write their autobiographies. Rousseau's publication of his life story was therefore a startlingly new endeavour that highlighted the importance for *everyone* of introspection, inwardness and the quest for self-knowledge. These qualities subsequently came to play pivotal roles in the construction of the modern sense of self-identity.[6] Encouraged by luminaries like Rousseau, we have come to appreciate the importance of following our own passions and talents in order to flourish (as epitomised by the metaphorical figure of the *Pathfinder* in the chapter on envy). Moreover, researchers like Asch have shown the dangers of *failing* to remain genuine and true to ourselves.

Many notable figures, not least Henry David Thoreau, the

renowned poet and philosopher, have followed this clarion call to authenticity and freedom of thought. In 1845, Thoreau famously 'went into the woods' to pursue a simple life in a small hut near Walden Pond over the next two years. (Although, admittedly, he did frequently visit his mother, who lived near by, to get his washing done!) Striving to 'live deep and suck out all the marrow of life', he immersed himself in his isolation and the stark beauty of nature. As such, he embodied the *Star Gazer*, whom we shall meet below. But his significance also lies in the independence of thought that he fashioned and asserted while living apart from society, and indeed continued to assert throughout his life. He was, for instance, a vociferous abolitionist who was particularly incensed by the 1850 Fugitive Slave Act. This required the Northern States – including his own, New England – to capture any slaves who had escaped from the South and return them to their 'owners'. Thoreau felt that citizens had a moral duty to refuse to participate in this state-sanctioned injustice. Consequently, he vowed to withhold his taxes until the law was repealed – a protest that Gandhi hailed as a model for his own passive resistance several decades later.

So, aloneness gives our inner *Free Thinker* the opportunity to take root, flourish and assert its independence. Meanwhile, it also provides the time and space for our soul to sing.

The Soul Singer

Ludwig van Beethoven was just twenty-six when he started to go deaf. Thereafter, the slow but inexorable descent into silence must have felt like a personal and professional catastrophe. Yet, rather than impeding his genius, musicologists have suggested that it may have enabled him to flourish and reach peaks that would perhaps have been out of reach had his hearing remained unimpaired. In the previous chapter, we saw that boredom's enforced spaciousness can spark creativity. Similarly, it seems that solitude may help us to coax inspiration from the shadows. It is as if, set apart from the world, we are able to hear the faint melodies of celestial music emanating from deep within – beautiful music that would be drowned out by the clamouring voices of the crowd. Beethoven's isolation – instantiated by his descent into deafness – allowed his creative genius to reach new, unprecedented heights. In the words of Martin Cooper, by the time the composer's deafness was total, he was in communion with himself, concerned only with the 'pure essence of his own thoughts'.[7] Similarly, in his wonderful book *Solitude*,[8] which provided much of the inspiration for this chapter, Anthony Storr reveals that Franz Kafka required total isolation in order to set his dark visions down on the page. As the wildly imaginative Czech author explained to his fiancé, 'writing means revealing oneself to excess ... That is why one can never be alone enough when one writes ... why even night is not night enough.'[9]

It is not only great artists who find that solitude is invaluable when they wish to express their deepest feelings and longings, though. We all have our songs to sing, and we may need to extricate ourselves from fear, embarrassment and obligation by leaving the crowd behind before we feel able to let our voices ring out. Indeed, Rousseau felt that society placed formidable constraints on self-expression. Some of these limits are necessary, of course: it is with good reason that we draft laws and develop norms to curtail our primitive instincts and inclinations. Civilisation would crumble pretty swiftly if everyone were able to indulge every passing whim. Yet, our societal proscriptions against self-expression go far beyond what is required to maintain order, frequently placing restrictive limits on even the most benevolent activities.

During my doctoral research, I focused on the impact of meditation on men's mental health. I recruited a terrific group of participants from a Buddhist centre and asked them for their life stories. I wanted to hear their narratives about why they had first tried meditation, and the effect it was having upon them. As a meditator myself, I expected them to extol the benefits of the practice, and indeed they did just that.[10] But I was much more struck by how difficult their lives had been *before* meditation.[11] We often hear that men are emotional vacuums, that they're not really 'in touch with their feelings'. Perhaps there is some truth in that, but research suggests it's more that males feel compelled to fulfil the *expectation* that they should be tough and stoical.[12] My interviewees vividly described the pressure they felt to live up to the injunction that 'boys don't cry'. Whether recalling their first day in secondary school, or the insistent demand to behave like 'one of the lads', they explained that suppression of emotions was part and parcel of daily life. They weren't 'allowed' to feel vulnerable, show affection or break down in tears. These 'rules' created an emotional straitjacket, gradually squeezing the life out of them. As a result, many of them experienced mental health issues as they struggled to deal with their repressed emotions. Some sort of resolution was found only when they turned, often in desperation, to meditation.

We shall travel further on these men's dark journeys in the final chapter, but the central point here is that restrictions on emotional expression can be extremely damaging. All of us are weighed down in one way or another by the burden of societal expectation, which prescribes how we *should* feel and act. Therefore, extricating ourselves from this can be rejuvenating. The participants in my research described the relief they felt when they were finally able to express their emotions, perhaps with a trusted partner. These precious moments were revitalising, as if a surging river had been undammed and was now free to rush towards the sea. This is the second great virtue of aloneness: it liberates us to express our deepest feelings and tear down the façade we usually feel we need to maintain for the eyes of the world.

Consider someone who sadly enters an enforced period of solitude. Far from the spirited *wanderlust* of the lone adventurer, this is the tragically more common case of someone who simply yearns for company – perhaps a single parent who watches the last of her children leave for university and is left alone in the family home. There is just silence and fading memories where once there was vibrant energy and youthful laughter. This may be a melancholic situation, but that's not necessarily *all* it is. The mother may reflect on her years of sacrifice, when she relegated her own needs and desires to provide for her family – the dreams and ambitions she set aside, the songs she was unable to sing, the books she was unable to write, the lands she could not visit. Perhaps it's so long since she heard her own inner voice that she's forgotten what it sounds like. Initially, then, the silence might be uncomfortable and unsettling, but as she starts to adjust and acclimatise, she may detect the first faint whispers of that voice, and in it the expressive individuality that has lain dormant for decades. This may lead to unanticipated adventures in which she finds new – or rediscovers old – passions or dreams. As she continues to lament the flight of her children, these dreams may bring at least some fulfilment to her days. In her loneliness, she may even find unexpected reserves of strength and courage. With this, we meet our inner *Fighter*.

The Fighter

I've always enjoyed solitary exercise. Just about every day I lace up my battered trainers and head out for a run along the rivers and canals of Oxford. This allows me to slip quietly outside the hustle of the city and enter into a different realm of existence, where I am alone with my freewheeling thoughts in the open spaces of nature. I get a glimpse of life from a different perspective and return home rejuvenated. Part of the appeal lies in testing my endurance, seeing how far or how fast I can go. I'm not a masochist – I don't push my body to the limit – but I do try to stretch my boundaries, curious as to where my stamina may take me.

Nevertheless, my brief forays into the world of endurance are inconsequential when compared to what some truly courageous and determined people have managed to achieve. For instance, I'm privileged to know a young woman who set herself the audaciously bold task of circumnavigating the globe entirely under her own steam. This included overcoming what must have been an overwhelming sense of vulnerability when rowing alone, mile after lonely mile, across the vast oceans. Indeed, she faced multiple near-death experiences as she floated perilously above the fathomless depths in a tiny craft that was not much bigger than a family car. On one occasion, twenty-metre-high waves capsized the boat in the middle of a violent tropical storm. Over the course of the journey she pushed her mental and physical endurance to the limit more times than most people do in a lifetime.

We often fail to appreciate the incredible resilience of the human spirit and forget that human beings are capable of astonishing acts of grit and determination. Take the staggering tale of Steve Callahan. He set out to cross the Atlantic in a twenty-one-foot sloop named – appropriately enough – *Napoleon Solo*. After a week, he collided with something in the water – perhaps a whale – and the sloop was holed beneath the waterline. Unable to patch the hole, Callahan launched his tiny, six-foot life-raft. It contained enough food and water to last him three days. A group of fishermen finally plucked him from the water, on the verge of death, after seventy-six days alone at sea in his little craft. During that time he had speared fish, made drinkable water with a solar still and patched up the raft when it was torn. Towards the end, it was all he could do just to cling on to life, but cling on he did. The Finns have a word for the extraordinary courage and determination we are able to muster in times of truly dire need: *sisu*. Callahan had *sisu* in spades, as does a refugee who marches for days through the desert in search of a safe haven, and people who battle through intense pain when they are struck by serious illness. Our will to live is fierce, and inspirational.

Enduring loneliness demands *sisu*. While Callahan's physical torment was extreme, his complete isolation may have been an even worse ordeal. Indeed, it is one of the cruellest hardships anyone can suffer. That is why so many regimes throughout history have imprisoned their critics and enemies in solitary confinement. The horrors of total deprivation of human contact run so deep that such prisoners often lose their minds. So it requires extraordinary mental determination to withstand this form of torture. But it *is* possible, as Dr Edith Bone proved.

A renowned linguist and translator, Dr Bone was entering her sixties, in the twilight of her career, when the authorities in Budapest detained her and accused her of being a British spy. They did not even bother with the pretence of a trial. Instead, they simply locked her away in solitary confinement for *seven years*, much of it spent in complete darkness in a dank basement. But she proved far tougher than her captors had ever suspected, and never buckled under their demands to sign a (false) confession. Determined to maintain her sanity, she kept her mind occupied throughout her confinement by mentally repeating poems she knew by heart and then translating them into other languages, compiling vocabularies and taking imaginary walks through the streets of familiar towns. In this way, she was able to emerge from captivity with her intellect intact. Her tale is heroic, and she is rightly lauded as inspirational – a prime example of *sisu* in the face of unspeakable hardship.

But *sisu* is evident in more common forms of isolation, too. Although these are far less extreme than Dr Bone's trials, they are nevertheless testament to human beings' incredible resilience. For instance, many older people endure significant loneliness as they approach the end of life. The privations of advancing age are well known: the slow loss of mobility, which renders socialising more difficult; watching friends pass away; the illnesses that keep people home- or hospital-bound. But there is little recognition of the sheer mental toughness that pensioners often display in the face of these hardships. Enduring the drawn-out trials of loneliness demands remarkable strength of character. As much as this may be painful, we may only hope that such people find some solace in the notion that they are fighting tough and staying strong.

Just as adventurers like my friend are driven forward by heroic single-mindedness – fighting off fear and quelling loneliness through sheer determination – we may hope to find the strength and resolution to complete our own missions, whatever they may be. Going further, when we are on these missions, we may find that solitude leads us into increasingly elevated planes of existence. Here, we meet the *Light Seeker*.

The Light Seeker

Deep in the Jordan Valley, some 250 metres below sea level, lies the town of Jericho, an oasis amid the dust of the desert, sweltering beneath the scorching sun. It is perhaps the oldest surviving human settlement on the planet, with traces of habitation dating back some eleven thousand years. It is like nowhere else on Earth, a place of extraordinary visions and mystical quests. It was here that Jesus was 'led by the Spirit for forty days in the wilderness', where he fasted and prayed in solitude, and where he supposedly battled with the Devil. The area still feels like a different plane of existence. The silence and solitude are almost frightening in their power. There are concessions to modernity – a rather incongruous cable-car trundles up the Mount of Temptation – but they don't detract from the austere grandeur of the nomadic land-scape. Indeed, for generations, lonely seekers have ventured into this barren wilderness. Some have even settled – high up the cliff face, carved into the rock itself, is the Monastery of the Temptation, which the Byzantines built in the sixth century AD. Beneath its ramparts is the cave where Jesus is said to have spent his forty days and nights in communion with the Spirit. *Light Seekers* continue to follow his example, Orthodox Christian monks who retreat to their cells, high above the world, in every sense. They are testament to the belief that the face of God may be glimpsed only through solitude, far from the multitude.

Just about every religious faith and spiritual tradition concurs with this view. Indeed, most of their scriptures contain accounts of their founders undergoing periods of isolation. For instance, the Buddha is said to have attained enlightenment after resolving to sit alone beneath a tree in the wilderness, and refusing to rise until he had achieved this supreme goal. Intriguingly, just like Jesus, legend has it that he remained there for forty days and was besieged by the forces of temptation, this time marshalled by Devaputra Mara, chief of all the demons. Meanwhile, in shamanic tra-ditions, the shaman – who is set apart from the rest of the tribe by some form of supernatural ability – disappears into the forest on vision quests that may last months on end. The world's spiritual traditions are united by their emphasis on the importance of solitude in the search for the sacred. As St Ignatius of Loyola, the sixteenth-century founder of the Jesuit movement, wrote in his *Spiritual Exercises*, 'The more our soul finds itself alone and isolated, the more apt it makes itself to approach and reach its Creator and Lord.'[13]

You may well think that the esoteric tales of the Buddha and Jesus are all very well, but they are merely relics of a bygone, mythological, pre-scientific age. The superhuman endeavours of these founders of the world's great religions might provide inspiration and comfort for their followers, but what relevance do they hold for the rest of us? In answering this question, my mind once again turns to the remarkable men I interviewed during the research for my PhD They generally had fairly standard upbringings, and most of them were pursuing routine careers: nursing, accountancy, teaching. Yet, Buddhism had transformed their lives. As I mentioned earlier, several of them had struggled with psychiatric problems, while others had been prone to alcoholism or aggression. Now, though, they were committed to the ideals of Buddhism – from abstinence to compassion – and were trying to reorient their lives around these values. Their lives weren't perfect, but they all said that meditation had made them far happier and more fulfilled. And yet, none of them felt compelled to don saffron robes, donate everything they owned to charity and disappear permanently to a mountain-top monastery in Tibet. Seeing them walking down the street, you would never know they were followers of Buddhism. They looked just like everyone else ... because they were. Except that they made an effort – in the midst of their busy lives – to set aside time for contemplative practice. This included going away regularly on retreat, where they were secluded from the world for days or even weeks on end.

Invariably, they described these retreats as highlights of their lives – although they could also be challenging – powerful opportunities to gain insight and illumination. (Encountering these insights, which sometimes included hard

200 • THE POSITIVE POWER OF NEGATIVE EMOTIONS

truths, was what made these retreats potentially challenging, albeit always greatly valued.) And I experienced something similar when I attended them, too. Initially, the prospect was daunting, especially the long periods of scheduled silence. Ultimately, though, those silent days were incredible. I never felt any sense of isolation. On the contrary, I was part of a group, yet liberated from the pressure to converse. This created the space for unhurried, beneficial self-reflection. For instance, the remote perspective allowed us to clarify and even resolve 'ordinary' problems back home. We are often so immersed in the minutiae of existence that it's difficult to see a solution. It's like wandering in a dense forest, struggling through the undergrowth, stumbling over tree roots. To extend the metaphor, a retreat is like being airlifted to a nearby hilltop, where we gain a broad view of the forest. We can see the false trails that lead to dead-ends, the concealed traps and hazards, and, above all, the path that heads straight to our destination. In other words, the solitude of a retreat can generate revelations that have the potential to transform life for the better.

Several of the meditators in my research group advocated going even further and spending months alone in some weather-beaten wilderness, where they reported coming face to face with their true selves and encountering the dizzying mystery of existence. Hence, they described these extended retreats as some of the most vital and treasured experiences of their lives, during which they were able to scale the otherwise inaccessible peaks of the human spirit and transform their vision of life and themselves. Afterwards, they would resume their regular lives with renewed energy and vigour (although some mentioned a jarring period of readjustment). For these were not retreats in the sense of 'escapes'. Rather, as expressed by the French aphorism *reculer pour mieux sauter* – step back in order to jump forwards – they served to propel these men onwards by allowing them to improve their lives.

Such prolonged withdrawals from society are impossible for many people, of course. But these meditators argued that even brief spells away from the crowd, alone with one's thoughts, can be edifying and illuminating. They also have the power to reconfigure how we relate to the world around us, as the final section in this chapter explores.

The Star Gazer

When Henry Thoreau ventured into the woods, his intention was not simply to develop his self-reliance. He was interested in more than whether he could build a rudimentary hut and catch a fish for his dinner. Nor did he subsequently make his name solely as an idealistic and eloquent critic of society, as important as that was. Rather, his legacy was built above all on his poetic reverence for the natural world. For it was Thoreau, together with Ralph Waldo Emerson, who created America's first home-grown intellectual movement: Transcendentalism. With growing alarm at the increasingly dehumanising industrialisation of the nineteenth century, the Transcendentalists exhorted their compatriots to abandon their unthinking conformity. Instead, they should discover 'an original relation to the universe', as Emerson put it. The Transcendentalists wished to cultivate profound respect and appreciation for the natural world. This went far deeper than simply admiring the scenery and promising not to step on delicate plants. It advocated a type of nature mysticism in which the world is revered as sacred. Indeed, these philosophers viewed the whole universe as a single mystical essence, with God in all things. As Emerson wrote, 'We see the world piece by piece, as the sun, the moon, the animal, the tree; but the whole, of which these are shining parts, is the soul.'[14]

Irrespective of whether we attain the esoteric heights of Emerson's spiritual philosophy, most of us have surely felt that magical sense of being in another world when we are alone in nature. It's as if, away from the magnetic presence of other people, quieter aspects of the world are able to emerge and reveal themselves in all their beauty. For example, in search of silence, we may flee the tumult of the city and escape to the unpeopled space of the countryside. Here, away from the constant hum of human activity – the conversations, the traffic, the radios and TVs – we find ourselves immersed in the quietude of the natural world. We may even feel a shiver down the spine. An eerie sensation often descends upon me when I'm running alone in the woods. It's as if I've entered a realm beyond civilisation, where human beings are superfluous, and more powerful, unseen forces are at work. The Earth suddenly feels far older than humanity, and I sense its confidence that it will far outlast our brief incursion into its territory.

This emotional state is probably best described as *awe*, which the psychologists Dacher Keltner and Jonathan Haidt have defined as being situated at 'the upper reaches of pleasure and on the boundary of fear'.[15] Philosophers of aesthetics have long been fascinated by this emotion, too. For instance, Edmund Burke devoted much of his attention to the notion of the *sublime*, and to the awe that phenomena possessing this quality are able to generate. He argued that we tremble before the sheer, inhuman power of the natural world: vast mountain ranges and volcanic eruptions created by relentless geological forces; roaring tides swept along by immense global currents; nuclear fusion at the heart of unfathomably large stars. All of this vastness overwhelms us, leaving us feeling like mere specks of dust inside a million-mile-wide tornado. Our admiration mingles with terror to produce respect, astonishment, even reverence. But it's not only the grandeur of power and vastness that precipitates awe. We may also become lost in wonder at the intricate miracles of nature, such as the minute, perfect symmetry of a tiny flower. As William Blake wrote so elegantly in *The Auguries of Innocence*:

> *To see a world in a grain of sand*
> *And a heaven in a wild flower*
> *Hold infinity in the palm of your hand*
> *And Eternity in an hour.*[16]

We are always liable to get caught up in the minutiae of our daily lives, tangled in the spiders' webs of our schemes and worries. It is only right and natural that we devote time and effort to the issues that create the substance of our lives, for without such attention we would soon cease to breathe. But we should also occasionally step outside our human concerns, gaze in awe at the stars, and wonder at the miracle of existence. Given all the burdens we carry, we *owe* it to ourselves to allow these moments of awe to enliven and lighten our lives. And it is only in solitude that we can truly step into this other realm. Awe tends to be dispelled by conversation, by laughter, even by the mere sight of other people. Our visions come crashing down to Earth, back into the human realm. So, whenever we are alone, perhaps we can scrutinise the natural world and allow its mystery to penetrate deep into our souls. We might continue to miss the company of others, but we can find solace in the thought that our solitude has granted us glimpses of beauty that we would otherwise have missed.

The *Star Gazer* epitomises the idea that we have explored in this chapter – namely, that we can transform the ache of loneliness into the tranquility of solitude. There is potential value in our aloneness, from the moral independence of the *Free Thinker* to the self-transcendence of the *Light Seeker*. This redemptive message has been our uplifting anthem through-out this book, where we've learned that all of our darker emotions can help us find the path to elusive happiness.

With that enticing possibility ringing through our minds, our journey is nearly at an end. It just remains to address suffering itself, which comprises all of the difficult feelings we have encountered on our travels. We shall see that there are healing sources of light even within suffering's oppressive darkness. We may be tested, wounded, even broken, but with care and grace we can hope to remake ourselves, and perhaps even emerge stronger and wiser.

CHAPTER EIGHT

Suffering

In this book we have travelled through some of the darker realms of human experience, through shades of melancholy and distress, agitation and concern. The path has not always been easy, but we have encountered some uplifting truths along the way. Chief among these is that, while some emotions are hard to bear, they can also be routes to happiness and fulfilment. Although each of these emotions feels unpleasant, they all possess unique forms of energy that we can learn to use to our advantage. They are like powerful trade winds blowing across the ocean of life, building in intensity as we try to stay afloat and reach our destination. They may knock us off balance at first, perhaps send us crashing to the deck. If they are particularly strong, they might even threaten to capsize us. Yet we can also learn to harness the dynamic force of the wind in our sails and use its power to carry us to a better place.

We began our journey by delving into sadness, which we

learned is an expression of love and compassion. It can be a form of self-preservation, protecting us from perilous situations by urging us to care for ourselves. And it becomes an expression of love when it encourages us to care for others. Sailing on, we encountered the tempest of anxiety – our natural warning system. We learned that its insistent siren can prompt us to initiate defensive strategies ahead of an impending crisis in order to avert or at least mitigate its impact. Next, we discovered that anger can be a moral emotion – a painful but illuminating sign that an ethic has been breached. We explored how, when harnessed skilfully, it may help us redress the iniquity that prompted our ire in the first place.

Whereas anger is often a sign that we have been wronged in some way, the next stage on our journey – guilt – usually indicates that we ourselves have erred. So we should heed its criticism, mend our ways and strive to become better people. Envy – our barometer of value – may induce a similar upward trajectory by urging us to pursue ever more elevated goals. Thereafter, we discovered that a garden of delights, insights and creativity may open up if we find the courage to venture deep into the rabbit hole of boredom. Similarly, our penultimate chapter suggested that we can transform the coldness of loneliness into the peaceful warmth of solitude.

So, our travels have taken us through seven realms, each with its unique shades and shadows, as well as its own precious beams of sunlight. But what of our journey as a whole, our trek through the darkness? Is there a larger arc, some overarching pattern, regardless of the individual route that each of us has followed? Indeed, there may be. The seven emotions in this book are but stars in the constellation of suffering. Whether we are sad, anxious, angry, guilty, envious, bored or lonely, we are suffering. It comprises all of these emotions and more. Indeed, we have not even touched upon many of the myriad hurts that afflict all human beings – from physical pain to social discomfort, from doubt to insecurity, from hatred to fear, from illness to death. All of these are also encapsulated within suffering.

We all suffer at least some of the time. No life is so blessed as to escape its talons completely. And, when we do, our suffering usually involves an infernal combination of the dark emotions listed above. We rarely travel through one emotional valley at a time. Whether battling illness or fighting for recognition, we may struggle with a multitude of emotional trials, such as a toxic brew of anger, sadness and envy, or a bitter draught of anxiety, guilt and loneliness. Moreover, our suffering may vary in both intensity (from mild discomfort to harrowing terror) and duration (from a few minutes to many years). Whichever route you have followed through the darkness, though, the whole journey goes by the name of suffering. With this in mind, we can return to the question that was posed above: is there an overarching pattern that holds true right across our disparate travails? As we shall discover below, there might well be. It is called the *Hero's Journey*.

Before we embark on that voyage, however, we need to explore the issue of suffering itself, through the metaphor of a *Shattered Vase*.

The Shattered Vase

In the battle-scarred aftermath of the Vietnam War, a new phrase entered the psychiatric lexicon: post-traumatic stress disorder (PTSD). As the veterans started to return from the front line, the medical staff back home noticed that their physical traumas were often healing faster than their mental scars. Indeed, for many of these veterans, the living nightmare of war simply did not end. They suffered horrific flashbacks of the hell they had endured, as if still in the midst of battle. A car backfiring may make them duck instinctively for cover and break out in a cold sweat. The ghosts of fallen comrades might haunt their dreams. Relationships became strained, as even the most sympathetic loved ones struggled to comprehend what the ex-soldiers had experienced. In the first half of the twentieth century, much of their suffering would have come under the rubric 'shellshock', which was used to describe the harrowed and hollowed-out state in which many traumatised fighters returned home from the two world wars. But that term had largely fallen into disuse by the 1970s, as the memories of those earlier cataclysms started to fade. So, with the publication of the third edition of the American Psychiatric Association's *Diagnostic and Statistical Manual of Mental Disorders* in 1980, the concept of PTSD was introduced to explain this type of lingering emotional turmoil.

Over the next few years, PTSD began to attract interest among clinicians and the public alike. It soon became clear that it was not limited to veterans, but could arise after any form of trauma – from serious illness, to natural disasters. At the same time, however, psychiatrists started to notice a less expected, parallel phenomenon: sometimes, after undergoing a severe trauma, survivors would report *positive* changes in their lives. By the mid-1990s, Virginia O'Leary and Jeannette Ickovics felt that trauma victims could be divided into *four* main categories.[1] Anyone who suffered drastically impaired functioning was described as 'succumbing'. If someone seemed able to pick up the threads of their life, albeit with those threads fraying and their grip faltering, they were said to be in a state of 'survival with impairment'. More fortunate were those who were deemed 'resilient'. They escaped from their trauma relatively unscathed and were able to return to their previous levels of functioning. Finally, a small percentage of survivors seemed to 'thrive', indeed sometimes even doing so *as a result* of the trauma they had suffered, achieving greater heights of functioning and fulfilment than they had experienced previously.

Unsurprisingly, this remarkable fourth group began to attract considerable attention. Before long, a bold new concept had made its way into the psychological literature, courtesy of Richard Tedeschi and Lawrence Calhoun: post-traumatic *growth* (PTG).[2] Moreover, even though this concept was inspired by survivors who were deemed to be 'thriving', researchers soon started to notice it in others, too. Even people in the other three categories might, in the midst of their suffering, experience some positive changes as a result of their trauma.[3] Indeed, studies have shown that up to 70 per cent of trauma survivors may benefit from the experience in some way.[4]

These tales of growth often share similar themes.[5] First, the survivors' relationships tend to be enhanced. There is perhaps nothing more powerful than trauma – a serious illness, say, or a traffic accident – to make people appreciate how much they need their loved ones. Arguments and grievances are often swept aside, paling into insignificance next to the thought of losing someone precious. Second, survivors frequently see themselves in a new, more positive light. For instance, they may feel a surge of courage and strength in the knowledge that they have overcome adversity. Third, a survivor may rewrite their personal philosophy in more uplifting verses. A brush with mortality tends to evoke increased appreciation of life, together with passionate determination to make every day count.

The psychologist Stephen Joseph employs a powerful metaphor to describe this process of positive change following trauma or adversity: the *Shattered Vase*.[6] When we suffer, some part of us always shatters. This can range from feeling as if our whole being has fragmented into pieces, to sensing that a single element has been broken – our trust in a particular person, say, or our confidence in a certain aspect of our character. So, what is the best solution? Think of a beautiful vase that you knock to the ground, shattering it into a thousand pieces. We might find it difficult to reassemble it into its former pristine state, and even if we managed to do so the result would probably be rather fragile. It is similarly challenging to resume life exactly as it was before a trauma: old habits and ways of thinking may no longer work. But what if we were to fashion a *new* work of art from the vase's fragments, a bold sculpture perhaps, or a vivid mosaic suffused with significance. It is this kind of refashioning that occurs during PTG. Although the elements of a person's life have been shaken and destabilised by the trauma they have suffered, they gradually – with time, patience and support – reassemble them in a new configuration. The new pattern does not necessarily eradicate the hurt, but it can contain understanding, meaning and sometimes even beauty.

Many empirical studies have explored and corroborated the phenomenon of PTG following adversity. It seems to provide great solace and hope for some trauma survivors, a light at the end of the dark tunnel. Yet Barbara Ehrenreich has warned that we must be wary of creating an *expectation* of it, and especially of implying that anyone who fails to enjoy such positive growth is deficient in some way. In her book *Smile or Die*, she vividly recounts her own experience of learning that she had been diagnosed with cancer.[7] As life-shatteringly awful as this diagnosis was, her suffering was then exacerbated by people who encouraged her – albeit with benevolent intent – to regard it as some kind of *positive* journey. I should point out that sensitive clinicians and researchers, such as Stephen Joseph, are careful not to impose such burdens on sufferers of trauma. But their nuanced understanding of the issue tends to get lost in more general cultural discourse, and especially in the language that is used when people contemplate and discuss serious illness. Some observers even implied that Ehrenreich should be *grateful* for her suffering, since it might be the gateway to personal transformation. Some illness survivors do indeed experience a sense of gratitude, but it is far from reasonable to tell all sufferers that they *should* feel it. For Ehrenreich, such advice simply added to her already heavy burden. In addition to suffering the trauma of her illness, she faced accusations that she was not a 'good' survivor. Her critics did not 'allow' her to feel angry or distraught, and she felt she could not rage against the brutalities of fate that had dealt her such a rotten hand. Instead, she was cajoled to find the 'benefits' and see the 'upside'.

I wish to avoid offering similar advice here. I hope that this book has shown that negative emotions have their place, and may even have significant value. But even if they cannot be put to positive use, they are entirely normal responses to the vicissitudes of life. We are not wrong to feel what we feel. So, when it comes to suffering, we ought to disregard anyone who says that we definitely will – or, even worse, *should* – experience some form of PTG. Numerous survivors and clinical research studies have shown that we *might* experience some positive changes. If so, that's wonderful. (Indeed, this chapter offers advice on how we may encourage this process.) But we all undertake our own unique journey through the darkness, and no one has the right to say how this will – or should – unfold. It is for this reason that I want to move away from the concept of PTG per se, and instead embark on the *Hero's Journey*.

Joseph Campbell, the great scholar of mythology, believed that all of the world's myriad legends were essentially variations on one great archetypal myth.[8] From the great epics of antiquity, such as Orpheus' descent into the Underworld, to contemporary classics, such as *The Lord of the Rings*, each grand narrative unfolds in a similar sequence of three broad acts: *Departure*, *Initiation* and *Return*. The fledgling hero (or heroine, of course, although these are much rarer in the older tales) receives an ominous and unsought 'call to adventure'. This precipitates a *Departure* from settled normality, a brave venture into the perilous unknown. Thus begins the *Initiation* – the hazardous journey itself, full of trials and tribulations, each of which tests the hero to the limit. These trials ultimately lead to revelation, with our hero reborn as a different person. This rebirth is the substance of the *Return*. Our hero has attained his elusive goal and so returns home, wounded and weary, but victorious and transformed.

These tales resonate so deeply with us because they provide a *redemptive narrative of suffering* and therefore offer solace and hope for anyone who has endured – or is enduring – hardship in their life. As such, the *Hero's Journey* traces the kind of trajectory that is seen in PTG, capturing it in powerful symbolic form, but it also encompasses every other survival trajectory. Sometimes simply staying alive, continuing to breathe, can be an act of great strength and heroism for those who have faced intense trauma.

However we fare in the aftermath of adversity, we are all on a *Hero's Journey*. Indeed, life itself is the ultimate such journey. Hence, this narrative has relevance for us all. When we suffer, it can help to see that suffering as a heroic quest, irrespective of whether we feel we are 'growing' as a result. Some of the trials might change us for the better. We may even feel that, in the immortal words of Friedrich Nietzsche, 'That which does not kill us makes us stronger.' With that in mind, let's begin with the *Departure*, the awful shattering of the vase.

The Departure

In November 1899, Hans Krása was born in Prague. At the time, Europe was brimming over with eager anticipation about what the new century might bring. With stunning progress in just about every field of endeavour – from medicine to physics, engineering to industry – there was every reason to believe that humankind's years of darkness lay safely in the past. Surely the world would soon be enjoying the fruits of increasing prosperity and innovation. No one could have foreseen that, within the space of just forty-five years, the planet would have suffered the trauma of two world wars, catastrophes of unprecedented brutality that shook

humanity's self-belief to the core. The second of these mael-
stroms ensnared and ultimately consumed Krása himself, as
it did millions of others, but until that point he dedicated
his life to beauty and the enrichment of the human spirit.
As a child, brought up lovingly within the Jewish faith, he
learned the piano and violin, then studied composition
at the German Music Academy. By the 1930s, his natural
talent was flowering into a wonderful career as a composer.
Then his world collapsed. He had just put the finishing
touches to a children's opera – *Brundibár*, based on a play by
Aristophanes – when, on 10 August 1942, the Nazis seized
him and transported him to the Theresienstadt ghetto. It
would be the last work he would ever complete.

It is difficult to comprehend the depths of inhumanity that
emerged in the Second World War. The brutality of the Nazis
and the other forces of fascism left an indelible stain on the
earth that will surely never fade. The hell of the ghettos and
the concentration camps surely represents the epitome of
human suffering, and just about the most traumatic experience a person could ever endure. Few *Departures* are as sudden
or as shocking as being forced at gunpoint into a ghetto or
onto a cattle train bound for a death camp. Separated in a harrowing instant from loved ones, probably never to see them
again. Suffering the theft not only of your home and possessions but of everything else that made you the person you are:
your culture, history, identity. Treated as subhuman, assigned
a number rather than a name, in a process that is specifically
designed to be as dehumanising as possible. The vase of each
and every victim was shattered in the most cold-blooded way
imaginable. Moreover, the Holocaust was the *Departure* writ
large, upon an unprecedented, earth-shattering, global scale.

Literally millions of victims were forced to undertake their own *Departures*. Indeed, humanity itself departed in those bleak years. Our self-image as a rational and humane species was undermined and threatened as never before. The largest vase of all – the earth – was shattered. Arguably, we are still trying to rebuild it.

But as deep and profound as the suffering was, tales of courage and dignity help us retain some faith in humanity. Moreover, many of the survivors went on to live great lives, testaments to the resilience of the human spirit. Some even experienced what we might now call PTG. These people could never forget the horrors they endured – they bore the physical and emotional scars their entire lives – but their suffering may have contributed to great insights and creativity that ultimately benefited all of humanity. Theirs were truly long and painful journeys, and it would be years, decades even, before they finally experienced some kind of *Return*. Even in the awful first phase of *Departure*, however, many of them were able to glimpse sources of light amid the enveloping darkness. Hans Krása, for instance, found solace in his love of music. This provided a precious connection to his past, his family, his culture, his identity. He still managed to see beauty in life and captured it in his music, composing several chamber pieces during his time in the ghetto. Moreover, he staged some fifty-five performances of *Brundibár*, with the cast consisting of the long-suffering children who were his neighbours. His is an empowering tale of 'spiritual resistance', and who knows what aesthetic and spiritual heights he may have reached had his life not been stolen from him. As it was, the Nazis ended his life in Auschwitz on 17 October 1944. Yet, he retained his humanity and his dignity right to the end.

Krása's story also highlights the importance of keeping alive some semblance of hope and meaning even as the vase starts to shatter. One of his fellow internees, Victor Frankl – one of the most influential psychologists of the twentieth century – was among the first to articulate this. Born in Vienna in 1905, he was just starting to establish himself as a psychiatrist when the Nazis transported him to Theresienstadt in 1942. Two years later, he was sent to Auschwitz, where he worked first as a slave labourer, then as a physician. The latter role led to a series of transfers to other camps, and to his survival, but by then the Holocaust had claimed his beloved wife, nearly his whole family and his life's work. (He had sewed the manuscript he had been working on for years into the lining of his coat, but the guards stole it and Frankl never saw it again.) Nevertheless, amid all the tragedy, Frankl formulated a powerful existential vision that would provide great solace to millions of people over subsequent decades. He realised that the inmates who felt they had something to live for were better equipped to withstand the horrors of the camps. For him, such people were potent affirmations of Nietzsche's maxim, 'If we have our own why of life, we shall get along with almost any how.'[9]

Frankl believed that one of the most powerful sources of salvation was love, even if – as in his own case – loved ones were lost. As he wrote, 'I understood how a man who has nothing left in this world still may know bliss, be it only for a brief moment, in the contemplation of his beloved.'[10] Out of such insights was born Logotherapy – 'healing through meaning'[11] – which Frankl developed after the war. This form of therapy involves guiding people to find some meaning and purpose in the traumas they have suffered, as

Susan – who lost her daughter Jill through the recklessness of a drunk-driver – did through her anti-drink-driving campaign (see Chapter 3). But Frankl's insights are helpful not only after the trauma has occurred – in the *Initiation* and *Return* stages – but *while* it is unfolding. He urged sufferers to search for a sliver of hope and focus on it, as this can serve as a lifeline when everything else seems hopeless. His personal lifeline was the memory of the love he had shared with his dear wife. The Nazis couldn't rob him of the fact that he had known deep, life-redeeming love, even though they stole everything else.

Whatever the circumstances of our own *Departure*, we may hopefully find a glimmer of light that gives us strength in the darkness. It may be no more than a kindly glance from a stranger, a friend's comforting words, a precious memory, or the hope of a better future, but that could be enough to provide a thread of salvation as we enter the trials of the *Initiation*.

Initiation

Ominously, taking his inspiration from the biblical story of Jonah, Joseph Campbell terms the final stage of the *Departure* the 'Belly of the Whale'. This metaphor evokes the deep descent into a seemingly hopeless situation before we miraculously make our way home during the *Return*. As such, the *Departure* ends when we cross the threshold into absolute darkness. At this moment we enter the second phase of the journey, when we face the ordeals of the *Initiation*.

Whenever I read about these notions, I'm reminded of a

friend who suffered a sudden descent into the belly of the whale from which it seemed that no *Return* would ever be possible. Mercifully, instead, the descent proved to be a great turning point in his life, the moment when his *Initiation* began. At first, however, he saw nothing but darkness, both metaphorically and literally.

He had skated on increasingly thin ice as a youth, drawn into the illicit thrills of taking and dealing drugs. Inevitably, the ice cracked: he was arrested, sent to prison and started his descent into oblivion. For a while he continued to deal, even while inside, supplying his fellow inmates with their fixes, but before long his illicit trade was discovered. At this point, his downward plunge accelerated, as he was placed into solitary confinement. As we saw in the previous chapter, this can be a terrible torment, and so it was for my friend, who recalls it as a living nightmare. As he lay alone on the mattress in a pitch-black cell, his fall seemed complete.

This kind of descent into a personal Underworld is relatively common, even though few of us will ever end up in solitary confinement for dealing drugs. To illustrate this, I'd like to return briefly to the group of meditators I interviewed during my doctoral research. Two-thirds of these men reported significant periods of suffering before taking up meditation, trials that brought them to a point where they felt they needed to change and find a better way of living. Most of them slipped into patterns of behaviour that are unfortunately all too common among Western men. Despite their emotional disconnection – or probably because of it – their inner worlds were in turmoil, whirlwinds of unregulated impulses and emotions. Many sought to anaesthetise their pain with drink or drugs. Others would throw themselves into their work. Some unleashed their pent-up emotional energy through random acts of aggression and violence. They had occasional moments in the sun – times of pleasure and happiness – but overall they painted a grim picture of the process of plunging into distress.

Then, at some point, would come the crash. Their ongoing suffering, and their dysfunctional methods of dealing with it, culminated in a moment of crisis, a tipping point that saw them careering over the edge into incarceration, drunken brawls that featured unsuspected peaks of violence, or the termination of a relationship. When such a relationship crumbled, many of these men felt as if they had nothing left. Some described hitting 'rock bottom'. A few came close to suicide. Their suffering was both desperate and familiar, given my own difficulties in the wake of the collapse of my first serious relationship (as I mentioned in the chapter on sadness). But all of these personal crises were genuine turning points. Although the path ahead was invariably hard, we all started travelling in a new direction that would ultimately lead to a better place. Rock bottom was the point when we realised with painful clarity that we *had* to change. As one of the meditators said, 'I was so done in that I just recognized it very plainly, "You need to do something."'[12]

This realisation of the need to change – to remake oneself – is the pivotal point of the *Initiation*. In this painful but redemptive second act of the story, we realise that the dark belly of the whale is a tomb where we 'die' and lose our old identity. Yet, it is also a womb where we are 'reborn' and resurrected. These two allegorical phases – death and rebirth – are intimately connected. We can progress to a higher stage of psychological development only if we abandon our old identity and move beyond it into a new mode of being. Ananda Coomaraswamy – the Tamil philosopher who was so influential in bringing Indian culture and thinking to the West – was fond of quoting St. Thomas Aquinas, who eloquently expressed this idea as follows: 'No creature can attain a higher grade of nature without ceasing to exist.'[13]

Take my friend, for example. He spent a life-changing week in solitary confinement. Haunted by ghosts of the past, the victims of his past misdeeds, he was tormented by confusion over how he had reached such an awful nadir. Then, after days of pain, buried beneath shame and regret, he spotted a faint glimmer of hope when he recalled his parents' unconditional love for him during childhood. Suddenly, he realised that he could live a different life: within the condemned man was an innocent soul. Clinging to this vague yet life-saving intuition, he began his slow, unsteady climb out of the darkness. In other words, he embarked on his *Return*.

The Return

During the *Return*, we begin the long, painful, but ultimately salvational process of emerging from the darkness and returning to the world. We are not yet healed, but we start to rebuild our lives, create ourselves anew. We take the broken pieces of the shattered vase and – often guided by the love and support of others – fashion them into a new creation that is imbued with meaning, significance and beauty.

There is a wonderful Zen Buddhist concept that has deep significance for us here: *kintsugi*. Although its origins lie in Buddhism, it has meaning for people of all faiths and indeed for those with none. Over the centuries, Zen masters have developed an unusual and very beautiful approach to broken crockery. Damaged items are neither neglected nor discarded; rather, they are mended with love and care whenever possible. This philosophy goes far beyond avoiding waste or frivolity. Nor is it about simply cobbling together fractured objects to make them functional again, or trying to reassemble the pieces so that the cracks are invisible. The word *kintsugi* is a compound of *kin*, meaning golden, and *tsugi*, meaning joinery. As this implies, the broken fragments are fixed together with a lustrous gold lacquer. Hence, the process involves *accentuating* the fault-lines in such a way as to render them beautiful and strong. Indeed, the cracks become the defining features of the object. The point is that these golden battle-scars are not flaws, but the essence of the object's character. They vividly express its depth and history in a poignant, resonant and, above all, beautiful way.

In the course of researching this book I read about many remarkable people who exemplify the notion of *kintsugi*, but I was particularly struck by the story of a young woman we'll call Claire. In her late teens, graced with rare talent and beauty, her life changed irrevocably when she was involved in a serious motorbike crash. In the hazy days and weeks that followed, lying heavily medicated in a hospital bed, initially she prayed that the surgeons would be able to rebuild her badly damaged face. But then she learned that no operations would be performed for at least a year, and thereafter the reconstruction would be a long, arduous process, with the strong possibility of permanent scarring. She wrestled with anger and hurt throughout that first year, barely leaving the house once she had returned home from hospital.

Nevertheless, once she had struggled through those dark months of *Departure* and *Initiation*, Claire gradually started to cultivate a spirit of bold defiance. She resumed a 'normal' life and refused to see herself as disfigured by her scars, casting off the idea that she should continue to cower in the shadows. Moreover, as her confidence grew, she realised that others were seeing the lines on her face as marks of character that signified her courage and strength. Meanwhile, they viewed Claire herself as heroic and inspiring, not to mention beautiful. There was no shortage of romantic attention, and a few years after marrying she was blessed with children. So it was that Claire rebuilt herself, metaphorically and literally. She did not disown or hide her suffering, but transformed herself into something that both she and others considered full of grace. As such, she is an evocative symbol of the redemptive power of *kintsugi*, the process by which we learn to embrace our fault-lines so that they cease to be flaws and become the unique features that make us special.

Indeed, everyone who has illuminated our journey through this book has been a testament to *kintsugi* in one way or another. Whatever the nature of their injuries, they learned how to make their scars golden and transformed their troubles into redemptive qualities. Consider Rumi, whose sorrow at the loss of Shams-e Tabriz inspired some of the most powerful poetry ever composed. Or Søren Kierkegaard, who understood that anxiety goes hand in hand with living life to the full. Or Susan, who overcame her anger towards the man who killed her daughter by working with him to warn others of the dangers of drink-driving, and thereby found redemptive purpose in personal tragedy. We saw how guilt prompted one of Milgram's 'teachers' to follow his conscience and protest against the Vietnam War. We learned that an inauspicious start in life can provide the rocket fuel to propel an envious dreamer to unexpected heights. We explored the use of boredom as a gateway to self-transformation, as exemplified by Bodhidharma meditating in a cave. We discovered the great depths of resilience and the invaluable independence that can emerge during periods of loneliness, as epitomised by Dr Bone and Henry Thoreau. Finally, in this last chapter, we saw how Victor Frankl drew on his own trauma to formulate Logotherapy, which has since helped countless people.

All of these people embarked upon, endured and eventually returned from their own *Hero's Journey*. Some negativity or suffering entered their lives, causing them to depart down a dark road. Yet, within that darkness, they were able to harness their own negativity in redemptive ways. As such, they transformed those negative emotions and experiences into positive virtues that allowed them to flourish. Guided by this process, they were able to refashion themselves and their lives by drawing on the very suffering that had tested them.

We may all undertake similarly redemptive journeys, and moreover harness the positive power of negative emotions to propel and steer us on our way. Although we all have our cross to bear, it can come to symbolise our self-transformation. Our negative emotions, which are so often denigrated as ugly scars, can become golden trails – sources of value, pathways to flourishing, and even beautiful virtues.

I hope that this book may offer some solace and companionship on the sometimes difficult road we all take through life, and help to illuminate your path, guiding you to a better place.

Further Help and Resources

Identifying Clinical Depression and Anxiety

This is a book about the 'normal' emotions that we all experience from time to time. It is not a study of mental illness, which usually demands clinical and/or therapeutic help. Of course, differentiating between 'normal' emotions and mental illness is not always straightforward. For instance, in Chapter 1, I suggested that sadness can sometimes cross the line into clinical depression.[1] That line marks the point where something has 'gone wrong' with sadness.[2] If you are worried that you may have reached that point, then I would encourage you to see your General Practitioner (GP) or an equivalent medical professional. He or she should be able to advise if what you are suffering does indeed constitute depression and recommend treatment, if necessary. In terms of recognising if you *may* have crossed the line – and so would benefit from contacting your GP – a useful starting point is the American Psychiatric Association's *Diagnostic and Statistical Manual of Mental Disorders* (*DSM*), which clinicians worldwide use to determine what constitutes a mental health disorder.

There are several aspects to the *DSM*'s definition of 'Major Depressive Disorder'. First and foremost, it states that a person *may* be depressed if he or she has suffered depressed mood or a loss of interest or pleasure in daily activities for a period of more than two weeks. Of course, everyone differs in their general temperament, but the key issue here is that the depressed mood represents a change from the person's 'baseline' (i.e. their usual, habitual state).

In addition to this overarching criterion, the *DSM* lists nine specific symptoms. If at least five of these are present every day (or nearly every day) during the two weeks of depressed mood, then a diagnosis of depression might be appropriate. The nine symptoms are:

- depressed mood or irritable most of the day, nearly every day;
- decreased interest or pleasure in most activities, most of each day;
- significant weight change or change in appetite;
- change in sleep (whether insomnia or oversleeping);
- change in activity (either bodily agitation or slowness);
- fatigue or loss of energy;
- feelings of worthlessness, or excessive or inappropriate guilt;
- diminished ability to think or concentrate, or greater indecisiveness; and
- thoughts of death or suicide.

I would encourage you to visit your GP if you have suffered some or all of these symptoms, even if it hasn't yet been for two weeks. They may not reach a diagnosis of depression, but their advice may still prove invaluable.

It is also worth consulting the *DSM* with respect to anxiety (and indeed if you are worried that you are suffering from any mental illness). Just like sadness and depression, anxiety can be regarded as an illness once it passes a certain point. The *DSM* uses the term 'Generalised Anxiety Disorder' (GAD) to cover all clinically significant levels of 'general' anxiety. (There are also more specific forms, such as '*Social* Anxiety Disorder' – debilitating shyness in which the anxiety specifically relates to social interaction.) A diagnosis of GAD is possible if a person experiences excessive anxiety and/or worry about a number of topics, events or activities 'more often than not' over a period of at least six months. More specifically, this worrying needs to be accompanied by at least three of the following symptoms before such a diagnosis may be reached:

- edginess or restlessness;
- greater fatigue than usual;
- impaired concentration;
- irritability;
- increased muscle aches or soreness; and
- difficulty sleeping.

As you can see, these criteria are hardly objective. There is no exact rule for determining what constitutes 'excessive', for instance. Therefore, as with depression, and with any potential mental illness, I would encourage you to visit your GP if you feel you may be suffering from GAD. He or she will be able to offer advice on any treatment that may be necessary.

As a final caveat, some people might experience many of the symptoms mentioned above (regarding depression and/or anxiety) yet feel that these are entirely appropriate responses to their current life circumstances, rather than the signs of an illness. For instance, someone who has suffered a recent bereavement may well experience all nine of the acknowledged symptoms of depression but view them simply as natural aspects of the grieving process. Indeed, there is much debate within psychiatry about whether these symptoms constitute aspects of depression if they occur in the context of a traumatic life event. The latest edition of the *DSM*, published in 2013, errs on the side of caution. It states that if the criteria outlined above are met, then a diagnosis of depression ought to be *considered*, regardless of contextual factors, such as bereavement. That said, if you are suffering through a traumatic experience, you may not feel that such a diagnosis is appropriate for you. Nevertheless, I would still encourage you to see your GP. He or she will carefully consider whether your suffering might be problematic or whether it is 'normal' and appropriate, and will advise and help you accordingly.

Additional Resources

The following websites contain helpful information regarding various mental health conditions and treatment options.

- www.mentalhealth.org.uk
- www.mind.org.uk
- www.sane.org.uk
- www.nhs.uk/livewell/mentalhealth
- www.rethink.org

Help and support are also available at:

- www.samaritans.org

The Samaritans can also be reached by phone twenty-four hours a day on:

- 116 123

Calls are free from within the UK and Ireland.

Notes

1   World Health Organization (2006). *World Health Statistics 2006.* Geneva: World Health Organisation. For a more recent commentary, see Kessler, R. C., Aguilar-Gaxiola, S., Alonso, J., Chatterji, S., Lee, S., Ormel, J. and Wang, P. S. (2009). The global burden of mental disorders: An update from the WHO World Mental Health (WMH) Surveys. *Epidemiologia e psichiatria sociale, 18*(1), 23–33.

2   I am drawing here on Jerome Wakefield's influential notion of disorder as 'harmful dysfunction', in which an emotion can be deemed a disorder if it is both harmful *and* dysfunctional. See Wakefield, J. C. (1992). Disorder as harmful dysfunction: A conceptual critique of *DSM-III-R*'s definition of mental disorder. *Psychological Review, 99*(2), 232–247.

3   Wolpert, L. (1999). *Malignant Sadness: The Anatomy of Depression.* London: Faber and Faber, p. 74.

4   à Kempis, T. (1418–1427/1952). *The Imitation of Christ.* (Trans. L. Sherley-Price.) New York: Penguin Classics.

5   The notion that sadness functions to prompt disengagement from harm was formulated by Eric Klinger. See Klinger, E. (1975). Consequences of commitment to and disengagement from incentives. *Psychological Review, 82*(1), 1–25. See also Nesse, R. M. (2000). Is depression an adaptation? *Archives of General Psychiatry, 57*(1), 14–20.

6   Thierry, B., Steru, L., Chermat, R. and Simon, P. (1984). Searching–waiting strategy: A candidate for an evolutionary model of depression? *Behavioral and Neural Biology, 41*(2), 180–189.

7   Barr, R., Green, J. and Hopkins, B. (eds) (2000). *Crying as a Sign, a Symptom, and a Signal.* Cambridge: Cambridge University Press.

8   Forgas, J. P. and East, R. (2008). On being happy and gullible: Mood effects on skepticism and the detection of deception. *Journal of Experimental Social Psychology, 44*(5), 1362–1367.

9 The founder of positive psychology, Martin Seligman, has written that 'meaning consists in knowing what your highest strengths are, and then using them to belong to and serve something you believe is larger than the self'. See Seligman, M. E. P., Ernst, R. M., Gillham, J., Reivich, K. and Linkins, M. (2009). Positive education: Positive psychology and classroom interventions. *Oxford Review of Education*, *35*(3), 293–311, at p. 296.

10 Tedeschi, R. G. and Calhoun, L. G. (1996). The posttraumatic growth inventory: Measuring the positive legacy of trauma. *Journal of Traumatic Stress*, *9*(3), 455–471.

11 Pirsig, R. M. (1989). *Zen and the Art of Motorcycle Maintenance*. London: Arrow Books, at p. 416.

12 Gibran, K. (1995). *The Voice of Kahlil Gibran: An Anthology* (R. Waterfield, ed.). London: Arkana, at p.167.

13 Rumi, J. (1998). *The Rumi Collection: An Anthology of Translations of Mevlâna Jalâluddin Rumi* (K. Helminski, ed.). Boston: Shambhala, at p. 228.

14 Lewis, C. S. (1988). *The Four Loves*. New York: A Harvest Book/ Harcourt Brace & Company, at p. 121.

15 Bauman, Z. (2013). *Liquid Love: On the Frailty of Human Bonds*. New York: John Wiley and Sons, at p. 6.

Chapter 2

1 Friedman, H. S., Tucker, J. S., Tomlinson-Keasey, C., Schwartz, J. E., Wingard, D. L. and Criqui, M. H. (1993). Does childhood personality predict longevity? *Journal of Personality and Social Psychology*, *65*, 176–185.

2 Barlow, D. H. (2002). *Anxiety and its Disorders: The Nature and Treatment of Anxiety and Panic* (2nd edn). New York: Guilford Press. See p. 104 for definitions of fear and anxiety.

3 Hadfield, C. (2013). *An Astronaut's Guide to Life on Earth*. London: Macmillan, at p. 54.

4 The first is: Kappes, H. B. and Oettingen, G. (2011). Positive fantasies about idealized futures sap energy. *Journal of Experimental Social Psychology*, *47*(4), 719–729. The second is: Kappes, H. B., Sharma, E. and Oettingen, G. (2013). Positive fantasies dampen charitable giving when many resources are demanded. *Journal of Consumer Psychology*, *23*(1), 128–135. The third is: Kappes, H. B., Oettingen, G. and Mayer, D. (2012). Positive fantasies predict low academic achievement in disadvantaged students. *European Journal of Social Psychology*, *42*(1), 53–64.

5 Kappes, H. B. and Oettingen, G. (2011). Positive fantasies about

idealized futures sap energy. *Journal of Experimental Social Psychology*, *47*(4), 719–729.

6　Kappes, H. B., Sharma, E. and Oettingen, G. (2013). Positive fantasies dampen charitable giving when many resources are demanded. *Journal of Consumer Psychology*, *23*(1), 128–135.

7　Kappes, H. B., Oettingen, G. and Mayer, D. (2012). Positive fantasies predict low academic achievement in disadvantaged students. *European Journal of Social Psychology*, *42*(1), 53–64.

8　Stadler, G., Oettingen, G. and Gollwitzer, P. M. (2010). Intervention effects of information and self-regulation on eating fruits and vegetables over two years. *Health Psychology*, *29*(3), 274–283.

9　Robinson, M. (2012). Titanic needed '50% more lifeboats' and had just six life buoys as new documents reveal astonishing cover-up of safety warnings. *Daily Mail*, 31 October.

10　Kierkegaard, S. (1844/1980). *The Concept of Anxiety*. (Trans. and ed. R. Thomte and A. B. Anderson.) Princeton, NJ: Princeton University Press, at p. 155.

11　Kierkegaard, S. (2000). *The Essential Kierkegaard* (H. V. Hong & E. H. Hong Eds.). Princeton, NJ: Princeton University Press, at p. 138.

Chapter 3

1　Tetlock, P. E., Kristel, O. V., Elson, S. B., Green, M. C. and Lerner, J. S. (2000). The psychology of the unthinkable: Taboo trade-offs, forbidden base rates, and heretical counterfactuals. *Journal of Personality and Social Psychology*, *78*(5), 853–870.

2　Cited in McLynn, F. (2011). *Marcus Aurelius: Warrior, Philosopher, Emperor*. London: The Bodley Head, at p. 588.

3　Eterovich, F. H. (1980). *Aristotle's Nicomachean Ethics: Commentary and Analysis*. Washington DC: University Press of America, at p. 40.

4　Ross, L. (1977). The intuitive psychologist and his shortcomings: Distortions in the attribution process. In L. Berkowitz (ed.), *Advances in Experimental Social Psychology* (pp. 173–220). New York: Academic Press.

5　Rozin, P., Lowery, L., Imada, S. and Haidt, J. (1999). The CAD triad hypothesis: A mapping between three moral emotions (contempt, anger, disgust) and three moral codes (community, autonomy, divinity). *Journal of Personality and Social Psychology*, *76*(4), 574–586.

6　Shweder, R. A., Much, N. C., Mahapatra, M. and Park, L. (1997). The 'Big Three' of morality (autonomy, community, divinity) and the 'Big Three' explanations of suffering. In A. Brandt and P.

Rozin (eds), *Morality and Health* (pp. 119–169). London: Routledge.

7   Kerby, S. (2013). The top 10 most startling facts about people of color and criminal justice in the United States. Fact sheet. Washington, DC: Center for American Progress.

8   DeNavas-Walt, C. and Proctor, B. D. (2015). *Income and Poverty in the United States: 2014*. Washington: United States Census Bureau.

9   Wollstonecraft, M. (1792/1990). *A Vindication of the Rights of Woman*. Buffalo, NY: Prometheus Books.

10   Office for National Statistics (2014). *Annual Survey of Hours and Earnings, 2014 Provisional Results*. London: Office for National Statistics.

11   Office of National Statistics (2012). *Measuring National Well-being – Health*. London: Office for National Statistics.

12   Ministry of Justice (2012). *Statistics on Women and the Criminal Justice System 2011*. London: Ministry of Justice.

13   Torres, E. (2015). Philippines murder highlights the threat facing trade unionists. *Equal Times*, 24 March.

14   Camus, A. (1956). *The Rebel: An Essay on Man in Revolt* (A. Bower, Trans.). New York: Vintage.

15   Neff, K. D. and Germer, C. K. (2013). A pilot study and randomized controlled trial of the mindful self-compassion program. *Journal of Clinical Psychology, 69*(1), 28–44.

16   Salzberg, S. (2004). *Loving-Kindness: The Revolutionary Art of Happiness*. Boston, MA: Shambhala Publications.

17   Institute for Global Labour and Human Rights (2014). Factory collapse in Bangladesh. Fact sheet. Pittsburgh, PA: Institute for Global Labour and Human Rights.

18   Grappi, S., Romani, S. and Bagozzi, R. P. (2013). Consumer response to corporate irresponsible behavior: Moral emotions and virtues. *Journal of Business Research, 66*(10), 1814–1821; Grappi, S., Romani, S. and Bagozzi, R. (2015). Consumer stakeholder responses to reshoring strategies. *Journal of the Academy of Marketing Science, 43*(4), 453–471.

19   MenCare (2015). *State of the World's Fathers*. Washington, DC: MenCare.

20   McNulty, J. K. and Fincham, F. D. (2011). Beyond positive psychology? Toward a contextual view of psychological processes and well-being. *American Psychologist, 67*(2), 101–110.

21   Lundahl, B. W., Taylor, M. J., Stevenson, R. and Roberts, K. D. (2008). Process-based forgiveness interventions: A meta-analytic review. *Research on Social Work Practice, 18*(5), 465–478.

22   Calhoun, L. G. and Tedeschi, R. G. (2014). *Handbook of Posttraumatic Growth: Research and Practice*. New York: Routledge.

Chapter 4

1   Zhong, C.-B. and Liljenquist, K. (2006). Washing away your sins: Threatened morality and physical cleansing. *Science, 313*(5792), 1451–1452.

2   Also reported in Zhong, C.-B. and Liljenquist, K. (2006). Washing away your sins: Threatened morality and physical cleansing. *Science, 313*(5792), 1451–1452.

3   Ronson, J. (2015). *So You've Been Publicly Shamed*. London: Picador.

4   Kohlberg, L. (1968). Stage and sequence: The cognitive-developmental approach to socialization. In D. A. Goslin (ed.), *Handbook of Socialization Theory and Research* (pp. 347–480). London: Rand McNally.

5   Maslow, A. H. (1943). A theory of human motivation. *Psychological Review, 50*(4), 370–396.

6   Jung, C. G. (1939/1963). *The Integration of the Personality*. (Trans. S. Dell.) London: Routledge and Kegan Paul.

7   Milgram, S. (1963). Behavioral study of obedience. *Journal of Abnormal and Social Psychology, 67*(4), 371–378.

8   Arendt, H. (1963). *Eichmann in Jerusalem*. New York: Penguin.

9   Tucker, A. W. (1983). The mathematics of Tucker: A sampler. *The Two-Year College Mathematics Journal, 14*(3), 228–232.

10 Ketelaar, T. and Tung Au, W. (2003). The effects of feelings of guilt on the behaviour of uncooperative individuals in repeated social bargaining games: An affect-as-information interpretation of the role of emotion in social interaction. *Cognition and Emotion, 17*(3), 429–453.

11 Baumeister, R. F., Stillwell, A. M. and Heatherton, T. F. (1995). Personal narratives about guilt: Role in action control and interpersonal relationships. *Basic and Applied Social Psychology, 17*(1–2), 173–198.

12 Mulder, R., Pouwelse, M., Lodewijkx, H. and Bolman, C. (2014). Workplace mobbing and bystanders' helping behaviour towards victims: The role of gender, perceived responsibility and anticipated stigma by association. *International Journal of Psychology, 49*(4), 304–312.

13 Waytz, A., Dungan, J. and Young, L. (2013). The whistleblower's dilemma and the fairness–loyalty tradeoff. *Journal of Experimental Social Psychology, 49*(6), 1027–1033.

14 Baumard, N. and Chevallier, C. (2012). What goes around comes around: The evolutionary roots of the belief in immanent justice. *Journal of Cognition and Culture, 12*(1–2), 67–80.

15 Hoffman, D., Carter, D., Lopez, C., Benzmiller, H., Guo, A., Latifi, S. and Craig, D. (2015). *Report to the Special Committee of*

the Board of Directors of the American Psychological Association: Independent Review Relating to APA Ethics Guidelines, National Security Interrogations, and Torture. Chicago: Sidley Austin.

16   Clay, R. A. (2016). Jean Maria Arrigo wins AAAS award. *Monitor on Psychology, 47*(4), 8.

17   Cosley, B. J., McCoy, S. K., Saslow, L. R. and Epel, E. S. (2010). Is compassion for others stress buffering? Consequences of compassion and social support for physiological reactivity to stress. *Journal of Experimental Social Psychology, 46*(5), 816–823.

18   Kim, J.-W., Kim, S.-E., Kim, J.-J., Jeong, B., Park, C.-H., Son, A. R. and Ki, S. W. (2009). Compassionate attitude towards others' suffering activates the mesolimbic neural system. *Neuropsychologia, 47*(10), 2073–2081.

19   Fredrickson, B. L., Cohn, M. A., Coffey, K. A., Pek, J. and Finkel, S. M. (2008). Open hearts build lives: Positive emotions, induced through loving-kindness meditation, build consequential personal resources. *Journal of Personality and Social Psychology, 95*(5), 1045–1062.

Chapter 5

1   Grolleau, G., Mzoughi, N. and Sutan, A. (2006). Do you envy others competitively or destructively? An experimental and survey investigation. Working paper.

2   Thomason, K. K. (2015). The moral value of envy. *Southern Journal of Philosophy, 53*(1), 36–53.

3   Maslow, A. H. (1968). *Toward a Psychology of Being.* Princeton, NJ: Van Nostrand, at p. 14.

4   In his earlier writings, Maslow identified only five levels. However, later in life, he began to feel that the fifth level – 'self-actualisation' – should be divided, giving rise to a sixth level: 'self-transcendence'. See Koltko-Rivera, M. E. (2006). Rediscovering the later version of Maslow's hierarchy of needs: Self-transcendence and opportunities for theory, research, and unification. *Review of General Psychology, 10*(4), 302–317.

5   van de Ven, N., Zeelenberg, M. and Pieters, R. (2009). Leveling up and down: The experiences of benign and malicious envy. *Emotion, 9*(3), 419–429.

6   Broughton, N., Kanabar, R. and Martin, N. (2015). *Wealth in the Downturn: Winners and Losers.* London: Social Market Foundation.

7   Helliwell, J. F., Layard, R. and Sachs, J. (eds) (2016). *World Happiness Report.* Geneva: United Nations Sustainable Development Solutions Network.

8   Schwartz, B. (2000). Self-determination: The tyranny of freedom. *American Psychologist*, *55*(1), 79–88.

9   Easterlin, R. A. (1974). Does economic growth improve the human lot? Some empirical evidence. In R. David and R. Reder (eds), *Nations and Households in Economic Growth: Essays in Honor of Moses Abramovitz* (Vol. 89, pp. 89–125). New York: Academic Press.

10 Easterlin, R. A. (1995). Will raising the incomes of all increase the happiness of all? *Journal of Economic Behavior and Organization*, *27*(1), 35–47.

11 Wilkinson, R. G. and Pickett, K. (2010). *The Spirit Level: Why More Equal Societies Almost Always Do Better*. London: Allen Lane.

12 Hyyppä, M. T. and Mäki, J. (2001). Why do Swedish-speaking Finns have longer active life? An area for social capital research. *Health Promotion International*, *16*(1), 55–64; Hyyppä, M. T. and Mäki, J. (2003). Social participation and health in a community rich in stock of social capital. *Health Education Research*, *18*(6), 770–779.

13 Reported in The Sun News editorial, Myrtle Beach, SC, 22 March 2014: Bestler, Bob. 'Words of Wisdom from Vonnegut.' Myrtle Beach, SC: The Sun News, 22 March 2014. Print. Cited in O'Connell, F. (2015). *Stuff I Wish I'd Known when I Started Working*. Chichester: John Wiley & Sons, at p. 61.

Chapter 6

1   Pirsig, R. M. (1989). *Zen and the Art of Motorcycle Maintenance*. London: Arrow Books, at p. 29.

2   Pirsig, R. M. (1989). *Zen and the Art of Motorcycle Maintenance*. London: Arrow Books, at p. 321.

3   Dickens, C. (1853). *Bleak House* (Vol. 1). London: Bradbury & Evans, at p. 6.

4   Hecht, J. M. (2013). *Stay: A History of Suicide and the Philosophies against it*. New Haven: Yale University Press, at p. 42.

5   Szasz, T. S. (2002). *Fatal Freedom: The Ethics and Politics of Suicide*. New York: Syracuse University Press.

6   Klapp, O. (1986). *Overload and Boredom: Essays on the Quality of Life in the Information Society*. New York: Greenwood Place.

7   Carroll, L. (2010). *Alice's Adventures in Wonderland*. London: Harper Press, at p. 1.

8   Iyengar, S. S. and Lepper, M. R. (2000). When choice is demotivating: Can one desire too much of a good thing? *Journal of Personality and Social Psychology*, *79*(6), 995–1006.

9   Sunstein, C. R. (2015). *Choosing Not to Choose: Understanding the Value of Choice*. Oxford: Oxford University Press.
10 Kierkegaard, S. (1834/1957). *The Concept of Dread* (2nd edn). (Trans. W. Lowrie.) Princeton, NJ: Princeton University Press.
11 Sartre, J.-P. (1952). *Existentialism and Humanism*. (Trans. P. Mairet.) Paris: Methuen.
12 Gladwell, M. (2008). *Outliers: The Story of Success*. London: Hachette.
13 Ericsson, K. A., Prietula, M. J. and Cokely, E. T. (2007). The making of an expert. *Harvard Business Review, 85*(7/8), 114–120.
14 Csikszentmihalyi, M. (1990). *Flow: The Psychology of Optimal Experience*. New York: Harper Perennial.
15 Cage, J. (1939). *Silence*. Hanover, NH: Wesleyan University Press, at p. 93.
16 Posner, M. I. and Petersen, S. E. (1990). The attention system of the human brain. *Annual Review of Neuroscience, 13*(1), 25–42.
17 Nietzsche, F. (1882/2001). *The Gay Science: With a Prelude in German Rhymes and an Appendix of Songs* (J. Nauckhoff, Trans. B. Williams ed.). Cambridge: Cambridge University Press, at p. 57.
18 Raichle, M. E., MacLeod, A. M., Snyder, A. Z., Powers, W. J., Gusnard, D. A. and Shulman, G. L. (2001). A default mode of brain function. *Proceedings of the National Academy of Sciences, 98*(2), 676–682.
19 Takeuchi, H., Taki, Y., Hashizume, H., Sassa, Y., Nagase, T., Nouchi, R. and Kawashima, R. (2012). The association between resting functional connectivity and creativity. *Cerebral Cortex, 22*(12), 2921–2929
20 Andrews-Hanna, J. R., Smallwood, J. and Spreng, R. N. (2014). The default network and self-generated thought: Component processes, dynamic control, and clinical relevance. *Annals of the New York Academy of Sciences, 1316*(1), 29–52.
21 Abraham, A. (2013). The world according to me: Personal relevance and the medial prefrontal cortex. *Frontiers in Human Neuroscience, 7*, 341.
22 Greicius, M. D., Krasnow, B., Reiss, A. L. and Menon, V. (2003). Functional connectivity in the resting brain: A network analysis of the default mode hypothesis. *Proceedings of the National Academy of Sciences, 100*(1), 253–258.
23 Schott, G. (2011). Doodling and the default network of the brain. *The Lancet, 378*(9797), 1133–1134.
24 Heller, J. (1955/2004). *Catch-22*. London: Vintage, at p. 43.
25 Heller, J. (1955/2004). *Catch-22*. London: Vintage, at p. 44.
26 Watt, J. D. (1991). Effect of boredom proneness on time perception. *Psychological Reports, 69*(1), 323–327.

27 Heidegger, M. (1938/2001). *The Fundamental Concepts of Meta-physics: World, Finitude, Solitude.* Bloomington: Indiana University Press.

28 Brodsky, J. (1997). *On Grief and Reason: Essays.* Harmondsworth: Penguin, at p. 109.

29 Osho. (2015). *The Great Zen Master Ta Hui: Reflections on the Transformation of an Intellectual to Enlightenment.* New York: Osho Media International, at p. 486.

Chapter 7

1 Tillich, P. (1963). *The Eternal Now.* New York: Scribner. Cited in Lionberger, J. (2007). *Renewal in the Wilderness: A Spiritual Guide to Connecting with God in the Natural World.* Woodstock, Vermont: SkyLight Paths Publishing, at p. 121.

2 Robinson, H., MacDonald, B., Kerse, N. and Broadbent, E. (2013). The psychosocial effects of a companion robot: A randomized controlled trial. *Journal of the American Medical Directors Association, 14*(9), 661–667.

3 Heidegger, M. (1927). *Being and Time.* (Trans. J. MacQuarrie and E. Robinson.) London: Blackwell.

4 Asch, S. E. (1956). Studies of independence and conformity: A minority of one against a unanimous majority. *Psychological monographs: General and Applied, 70*(9), 1–70.

5 Rousseau, J.-J. (1782/1953). *Confessions.* (Trans. J. M. Cohen.) Baltimore, MD: Penguin.

6 Taylor, C. (1989). *Sources of the Self: The Making of the Modern Identity.* Cambridge, MA: Harvard University Press.

7 Cooper, M. (1970). *Beethoven: The Last Decade.* London: Oxford University Press, at p. 11.

8 Storr, A. (1989). *Solitude.* London: Flamingo.

9 Kafka, F. (1974). *Letters to Felice.* (Trans. J. Stern and E. Duckworth; eds E. Heller and J. Born.) London: Vintage, at pp. 155–156.

10 Lomas, T., Cartwright, T., Edginton, T. and Ridge, D. (2014). A religion of wellbeing? The appeal of Buddhism to men in London, UK. *Psychology of Religion and Spirituality, 6*(3), 198–207.

11 Lomas, T., Cartwright, T., Edginton, T. and Ridge, D. (2013). 'I was so done in that I just recognized it very plainly, "You need to do something"': Men's narratives of struggle, distress and turning to meditation. *Health, 17*(2), 191–208.

12 Connell, R. W. (1995). *Masculinities.* Berkeley: University of California Press.

13 Saint Ignatius of Loyola (2012). *Saint Ignatius: The Spiritual*

Writings. Selections Annotated and Explained (M. Mossa, ed.). Woodstock, Vermont: Skylight Paths Publishing, at p. 61.

14 Emerson, R. W. (1987). *The Essays of Ralph Waldo Emerson* (A. R. Ferguson & J. F. Carr, eds). Boston: Harvard University Press, at p. 160

15 Keltner, D. and Haidt, J. (2003). Approaching awe, a moral, spiritual, and aesthetic emotion. *Cognition and Emotion, 17*(2), 297–314, at p. 297.

16 Blake, W. (1863/2000). *Selected Poetry and Prose* (D. Fuller, ed.). Harlow, England: Longman, at p. 285.

Chapter 8

1 O'Leary, V. E. and Ickovics, J. R. (1994). Resilience and thriving in response to challenge: An opportunity for a paradigm shift in women's health. *Women's Health, 1*(2), 121–142.

2 Tedeschi, R. G. and Calhoun, L. G. (1996). The Posttraumatic Growth Inventory: Measuring the positive legacy of trauma. *Journal of Traumatic Stress, 9*(3), 455–471.

3 Calhoun, L. G. and Tedeschi, R. G. (2014). *Handbook of Posttraumatic Growth: Research and Practice.* New York: Routledge.

4 Linley, P. A. and Joseph, S. (2004). Positive change processes following trauma and adversity: A review of the empirical literature. *Journal of Traumatic Stress, 17*, 11–22.

5 Joseph, S. (2012). *What Doesn't Kill Us: The New Psychology of Posttraumatic Growth.* London: Piatkus.

6 Joseph, S. (2012). *What Doesn't Kill Us: The New Psychology of Posttraumatic Growth.* London: Piatkus.

7 Ehrenreich, B. (2009). *Smile or Die: How Positive Thinking Fooled America and the World.* London: Granta.

8 Campbell, J. (1949). *The Hero with a Thousand Faces.* Novato, CA: New World Library.

9 Nietzsche, F. (1888/1976). Twilight of the idols. In W. Kaufmann (ed.), *The Portable Nietzsche.* New York: Penguin, at p. 468.

10 Frankl, V. E. (1963). *Man's Search for Meaning: An Introduction to Logotherapy.* New York: Washington Square Press, at p. 69.

11 Southwick, S. M., Gilmartin, R., Mcdonough, P. and Morrissey, P. (2006). Logotherapy as an adjunctive treatment for chronic combat-related PTSD: A meaning-based intervention. *American Journal of Psychotherapy, 60*(2), 161–174.

12 Lomas, T., Cartwright, T., Edginton, T. and Ridge, D. (2013). 'I was so done in that I just recognized it very plainly, "You need to do something"': Men's narratives of struggle, distress and turning to meditation. *Health, 17*(2), 191–208.

13 Aquinas, S. T. (1273/1981). *Summa Theologia*, 1. 63. 3. Cited in Coomaraswamy, A. K. (1988). *Selected letters of Ananda K. Coomaraswamy* (A. Moore, ed.). Delhi: Oxford University Press, at p. 155.

Further Resources

1 I am drawing here on Jerome Wakefield's influential notion of disorder as 'harmful dysfunction', in which an emotion can be deemed a disorder if it is both harmful and dysfunctional. See Wakefield, J. C. (1992). Disorder as harmful dysfunction: A conceptual critique of *DSM-III-R*'s definition of mental disorder. *Psychological Review, 99*(2), 232–247.

2 Wolpert, L. (1999). *Malignant Sadness: The Anatomy of Depression*. London: Faber and Faber.

Bibliography

Books

à Kempis, T. (1418–1427/1952). *The Imitation of Christ.* (Trans. L. Sherley-Price.) New York: Penguin Classics.

Arendt, H. (1963). *Eichmann in Jerusalem.* New York: Penguin.

Barlow, D. H. (2002). *Anxiety and Its Disorders: The Nature and Treatment of Anxiety and Panic* (2nd edn). New York: Guilford Press.

Barr, R., Green, J. and Hopkins, B. (eds) (2000). *Crying as a Sign, a Symptom, and a Signal.* Cambridge: Cambridge University Press.

Bauman, Z. (2013). *Liquid Love: On the Frailty of Human Bonds.* New York: John Wiley and Sons.

Blake, W. (1863/2000). *Selected Poetry and Prose* (D. Fuller, ed.). Harlow, England: Longman, at p. 285.

Brodsky, J. (1997). *On Grief and Reason: Essays.* Harmondsworth: Penguin.

Cage, J. (1939). *Silence.* Hanover, NH: Wesleyan University Press.

Calhoun, L. G. and Tedeschi, R. G. (2014). *Handbook of Posttraumatic Growth: Research and Practice.* New York: Routledge.

Camus, A. (1956). *The Rebel: An Essay on Man in Revolt* (A. Bower, trans.). New York: Vintage.

Carroll, L. (2010). *Alice's Adventures in Wonderland.* London: Harper Press.

Connell, R. W. (1995). *Masculinities.* Berkeley: University of California Press.

Coomaraswamy, A. K. (1988). *Selected letters of Ananda K. Coomaraswamy* (A. Moore, ed.). Delhi: Oxford University Press.

Cooper, M. (1970). *Beethoven: The Last Decade.* London: Oxford University Press.

Csikszentmihalyi, M. (1990). *Flow: The Psychology of Optimal Experience.* New York: Harper Perennial.

Dickens, C. (1853). *Bleak House* (Vol. 1). London: Bradbury & Evans.

Ehrenreich, B. (2009). *Smile or Die: How Positive Thinking Fooled America and the World.* London: Granta.

Emerson, R. W. (1987). *The Essays of Ralph Waldo Emerson* (A. R. Ferguson & J. F. Carr, eds). Boston: Harvard University Press.

Eterovich, F. H. (1980). *Aristotle's Nicomachean Ethics: Commentary and Analysis.* Washington DC: University Press of America.

Frankl, V. E. (1963). *Man's Search for Meaning: An Introduction to Logotherapy.* New York: Washington Square Press.

Gibran, K. (1995). *The Voice of Kahlil Gibran: An Anthology* (R. Waterfield, ed.). London: Arkana.

Gladwell, M. (2008). *Outliers: The Story of Success.* London: Hachette.

Hadfield, C. (2013). *An Astronaut's Guide to Life on Earth.* London: Macmillan.

Hecht, J. M. (2013). *Stay: A History of Suicide and the Philosophies against it.* New Haven: Yale University Press.

Heidegger, M. (1927). *Being and Time.* (J. MacQuarrie and E. Robinson, trans.) London: Blackwell.

Heidegger, M. (1938/2001). *The Fundamental Concepts of Metaphysics: World, Finitude, Solitude.* Bloomington: Indiana University Press.

Heller, J. (1955/2004). *Catch-22.* London: Vintage.

Joseph, S. (2012). *What Doesn't Kill Us: The New Psychology of Posttraumatic Growth.* London: Piatkus.

Jung, C. G. (1939/1963). *The Integration of the Personality.* (S. Dell, trans.) London: Routledge and Kegan Paul.

Kafka, F. (1974). *Letters to Felice.* (J. Stern and E. Duckworth, trans; E. Heller and J. Born, eds,) London: Vintage.

Kierkegaard, S. (1834/1957). *The Concept of Dread* (2nd edn). (W. Lowrie, trans.) Princeton, NJ: Princeton University Press.

Kierkegaard, S. (1944/1980). *The Concept of Anxiety* (R. Thomte and A. B. Anderson, trans. and ed. .) Princeton, NJ: Princeton University Press.

Kierkegaard, S. (2000). *The Essential Kierkegaard* (H. V. Hong and E. H. Hong, eds.). Princeton, NJ: Princeton University Press.

Klapp, O. (1986). *Overload and Boredom: Essays on the Quality of Life in the Information Society.* New York: Greenwood Place.

Lewis, C. S. (1988). *The Four Loves.* New York: A Harvest Book/ Harcourt Brace & Company.

Lionberger, J. (2007). *Renewal in the Wilderness: A Spiritual Guide to Connecting with God in the Natural World.* Woodstock, Vermont: SkyLight Paths Publishing.

Maslow, A. H. (1968). *Toward a Psychology of Being.* Princeton, NJ: Van Nostrand

McLynn, F. (2011). *Marcus Aurelius: Warrior, Philosopher, Emperor.* London: The Bodley Head.

Nietzsche, F. (1888/1976). Twilight of the idols. In W. Kaufmann (ed.), *The Portable Nietzsche.* New York: Penguin.

Nietzsche, F. (1882/2001). *The Gay Science: With a Prelude in German Rhymes and an Appendix of Songs* (J. Nauckhoff, trans.; B. Williams, ed.). Cambridge: Cambridge University Press.

O'Connell, F. (2015). *Stuff I Wish I'd Known when I Started Working.* Chichester: John Wiley & Sons.

Osho. (2015). *The Great Zen Master Ta Hui: Reflections on the Transformation of an Intellectual to Enlightenment.* New York: Osho Media International.

Pirsig, R. M. (1989). *Zen and the Art of Motorcycle Maintenance.* London: Arrow Books.

Ronson, J. (2015). *So You've Been Publicly Shamed.* London: Picador.

Rousseau, J.-J. (1782/1953). *Confessions.* (J. M. Cohen, trans. .) Baltimore, MD: Penguin.

Rumi, J. (1998). *The Rumi Collection: An Anthology of Translations of Mevlâna Jalâluddin Rumi* (K. Helminski, ed.). Boston: Shambhala.

Saint Ignatius of Loyola (2012). *Saint Ignatius: The Spiritual Writings. Selections Annotated and Explained* (M. Mossa, ed.). Woodstock, Vermont: Skylight Paths Publishing.

Salzberg, S. (2004). *Loving-Kindness: The Revolutionary Art of Happiness.* Boston, MA: Shambhala Publications.

Sartre, J.-P. (1952). *Existentialism and Humanism.* (P. Mairet, trans.) Paris: Methuen.

Storr, A. (1989). *Solitude.* London: Flamingo.

Sunstein, C. R. (2015). *Choosing Not to Choose: Understanding the Value of Choice.* Oxford: Oxford University Press.

Szasz, T. S. (2002). *Fatal Freedom: The Ethics and Politics of Suicide*. New York: Syracuse University Press.

Taylor, C. (1989). *Sources of the Self: The Making of the Modern Identity*. Cambridge, MA: Harvard University Press.

Tillich, P. (1963). *The Eternal Now*. New York: Scribner.

Wilkinson, R. G. and Pickett, K. (2010). *The Spirit Level: Why More Equal Societies Almost Always Do Better*. London: Allen Lane.

Wollstonecraft, M. (1792/1990). *A Vindication of the Rights of Woman*. Buffalo, NY: Prometheus Books.

Wolpert, L. (1999). *Malignant Sadness: The Anatomy of Depression*. London: Faber and Faber.

Articles, Chapters and Reports

Abraham, A. (2013). The world according to me: Personal relevance and the medial prefrontal cortex. *Frontiers in Human Neuroscience, 7*, 341.

Andrews-Hanna, J. R., Smallwood, J. and Spreng, R. N. (2014). The default network and self-generated thought: Component processes, dynamic control, and clinical relevance. *Annals of the New York Academy of Sciences, 1316*(1), 29–52.

Asch, S. E. (1956). Studies of independence and conformity: A minority of one against a unanimous majority. *Psychological Monographs: General and Applied, 70*(9), 1–70.

Baumard, N. and Chevallier, C. (2012). What goes around comes around: The evolutionary roots of the belief in immanent justice. *Journal of Cognition and Culture, 12*(1–2), 67–80.

Baumeister, R. F., Stillwell, A. M. and Heatherton, T. F. (1995). Personal narratives about guilt: Role in action control and interpersonal relationships. *Basic and Applied Social Psychology*, *17*(1–2), 173–198.

Bestler, Bob (2014) 'Words of Wisdom from Vonnegut.' Myrtle Beach, SC: The Sun News, 22 March 2014.

Broughton, N., Kanabar, R. and Martin, N. (2015). *Wealth in the Downturn: Winners and Losers*. London: Social Market Foundation.

Clay, R. A. (2016). Jean Maria Arrigo wins AAAS award. *Monitor on Psychology*, *47*(4), 8.

Cosley, B. J., McCoy, S. K., Saslow, L. R. and Epel, E. S. (2010). Is compassion for others stress buffering? Consequences of compassion and social support for physiological reactivity to stress. *Journal of Experimental Social Psychology*, *46*(5), 816–823.

DeNavas-Walt, C. and Proctor, B. D. (2015). *Income and Poverty in the United States: 2014*. Washington, DC: United States Census Bureau.

Easterlin, R. A. (1974). Does economic growth improve the human lot? Some empirical evidence. In R. David and R. Reder (eds), *Nations and Households in Economic Growth: Essays in Honor of Moses Abramovitz* (Vol. 89, pp. 89–125). New York: Academic Press.

Easterlin, R. A. (1995). Will raising the incomes of all increase the happiness of all? *Journal of Economic Behavior and Organization*, *27*(1), 35–47.

Ericsson, K. A., Prietula, M. J. and Cokely, E. T. (2007). The making of an expert. *Harvard Business Review*, *85*(7/8), 114–120.

Forgas, J. P. and East, R. (2008). On being happy and gullible: Mood effects on skepticism and the detection of deception. *Journal of Experimental Social Psychology*, *44*(5), 1362–1367.

Fredrickson, B. L., Cohn, M. A., Coffey, K. A., Pek, J. and Finkel, S. M. (2008). Open hearts build lives: Positive emotions, induced through loving-kindness meditation, build consequential personal resources. *Journal of Personality and Social Psychology, 95*(5), 1045–1062.

Friedman, H. S., Tucker, J. S., Tomlinson-Keasey, C., Schwartz, J. E., Wingard, D. L. and Criqui, M. H. (1993). Does childhood personality predict longevity? *Journal of Personality and Social Psychology, 65*, 176–185.

Grappi, S., Romani, S. and Bagozzi, R. P. (2013). Consumer response to corporate irresponsible behavior: Moral emotions and virtues. *Journal of Business Research, 66*(10), 1814–1821.

Grappi, S., Romani, S. and Bagozzi, R. (2015). Consumer stakeholder responses to reshoring strategies. *Journal of the Academy of Marketing Science, 43*(4), 453–471.

Greicius, M. D., Krasnow, B., Reiss, A. L. and Menon, V. (2003). Functional connectivity in the resting brain: A network analysis of the default mode hypothesis. *Proceedings of the National Academy of Sciences, 100*(1), 253–258.

Grolleau, G., Mzoughi, N. and Sutan, A. (2006). Do you envy others competitively or destructively? An experimental and survey investigation. Working paper.

Helliwell, J. F., Layard, R. and Sachs, J. (eds) (2016). *World Happiness Report*. Geneva: United Nations Sustainable Development Solutions Network.

Hoffman, D., Carter, D., Lopez, C., Benzmiller, H., Guo, A., Latifi, S. and Craig, D. (2015). *Report to the Special Committee of the Board of Directors of the American Psychological Association: Independent Review Relating to APA Ethics Guidelines, National Security Interrogations, and Torture*. Chicago: Sidley Austin.

Hyyppä, M. T. and Mäki, J. (2001). Why do Swedish-speaking Finns have longer active life? An area for social capital research. *Health Promotion International*, *16*(1), 55–64.

Institute for Global Labour and Human Rights (2014). Factory collapse in Bangladesh. Fact sheet. Pittsburgh, PA: Institute for Global Labour and Human Rights.

Iyengar, S. S. and Lepper, M. R. (2000). When choice is demotivating: Can one desire too much of a good thing? *Journal of Personality and Social Psychology*, *79*(6), 995–1006.

Kappes, H. B. and Oettingen, G. (2011). Positive fantasies about idealized futures sap energy. *Journal of Experimental Social Psychology*, *47*(4), 719–729.

Kappes, H. B., Oettingen, G. and Mayer, D. (2012). Positive fantasies predict low academic achievement in disadvantaged students. *European Journal of Social Psychology*, *42*(1), 53–64.

Kappes, H. B., Sharma, E. and Oettingen, G. (2013). Positive fantasies dampen charitable giving when many resources are demanded. *Journal of Consumer Psychology*, *23*(1), 128–135.

Keltner, D. and Haidt, J. (2003). Approaching awe, a moral, spiritual, and aesthetic emotion. *Cognition and Emotion*, *17*(2), 297–314.

Kerby, S. (2013). The top 10 most startling facts about people of color and criminal justice in the United States. Fact sheet. Washington, DC: Center for American Progress.

Kessler, R. C., Aguilar-Gaxiola, S., Alonso, J., Chatterji, S., Lee, S., Ormel, J. and Wang, P. S. (2009). The global burden of mental disorders: An update from the WHO World Mental Health (WMH) Surveys. *Epidemiologia e psichiatria sociale*, *18*(1), 23–33.

Ketelaar, T. and Tung Au, W. (2003). The effects of feelings of guilt on the behaviour of uncooperative individuals in repeated social bargaining games: An affect-as-information interpretation of the role of emotion in social interaction. *Cognition and Emotion, 17*(3), 429–453.

Kim, J.-W., Kim, S.-E., Kim, J.-J., Jeong, B., Park, C.-H., Son, A. R. and Ki, S. W. (2009). Compassionate attitude towards others' suffering activates the mesolimbic neural system. *Neuropsychologia, 47*(10), 2073–2081.

Klinger, E. (1975). Consequences of commitment to and disengagement from incentives. *Psychological Review, 82*(1), 1–25.

Kohlberg, L. (1968). Stage and sequence: The cognitive-developmental approach to socialization. In D. A. Goslin (ed.), *Handbook of Socialization Theory and Research* (pp. 347–480). London: Rand McNally.

Koltko-Rivera, M. E. (2006). Rediscovering the later version of Maslow's hierarchy of needs: Self-transcendence and opportunities for theory, research, and unification. *Review of General Psychology, 10*(4), 302–317.

Linley, P. A. and Joseph, S. (2004). Positive change processes following trauma and adversity: A review of the empirical literature. *Journal of Traumatic Stress, 17*, 11–22.

Lomas, T., Cartwright, T., Edginton, T. and Ridge, D. (2013). 'I was so done in that I just recognized it very plainly, "You need to do something"': Men's narratives of struggle, distress and turning to meditation. *Health, 17*(2), 191–208.

Lomas, T., Cartwright, T., Edginton, T. and Ridge, D. (2014). A religion of wellbeing? The appeal of Buddhism to men in London, UK. *Psychology of Religion and Spirituality, 6*(3), 198–207.

Lundahl, B. W., Taylor, M. J., Stevenson, R. and Roberts, K. D. (2008). Process-based forgiveness interventions: A meta-analytic review. *Research on Social Work Practice, 18*(5), 465–478.

Maslow, A. H. (1943). A theory of human motivation. *Psychological Review, 50*(4), 370–396.

McNulty, J. K. and Fincham, F. D. (2011). Beyond positive psychology? Toward a contextual view of psychological processes and well-being. *American Psychologist, 67*(2), 101–110.

Milgram, S. (1963). Behavioral study of obedience. *Journal of Abnormal and Social Psychology, 67*(4), 371–378.

Ministry of Justice (2012). *Statistics on Women and the Criminal Justice System 2011*. London: Ministry of Justice.

Mulder, R., Pouwelse, M., Lodewijkx, H. and Bolman, C. (2014). Workplace mobbing and bystanders' helping behaviour towards victims: The role of gender, perceived responsibility and anticipated stigma by association. *International Journal of Psychology, 49*(4), 304–312.

Neff, K. D. and Germer, C. K. (2013). A pilot study and randomized controlled trial of the mindful self-compassion program. *Journal of Clinical Psychology, 69*(1), 28–44.

Nesse, R. M. (2000). Is depression an adaptation? *Archives of General Psychiatry, 57*(1), 14–20.

Office for National Statistics (2012). *Measuring National Well-being – Health*. London: Office for National Statistics.

Office for National Statistics (2014). *Annual Survey of Hours and Earnings, 2014 Provisional Results*. London: Office for National Statistics.

O'Leary, V. E. and Ickovics, J. R. (1994). Resilience and thriving in response to challenge: An opportunity for a paradigm shift in women's health. *Women's Health*, *1*(2), 121–142.

Posner, M. I. and Petersen, S. E. (1990). The attention system of the human brain. *Annual Review of Neuroscience*, *13*(1), 25–42.

Raichle, M. E., MacLeod, A. M., Snyder, A. Z., Powers, W. J., Gusnard, D. A. and Shulman, G. L. (2001). A default mode of brain function. *Proceedings of the National Academy of Sciences*, *98*(2), 676–682.

Robinson, H., MacDonald, B., Kerse, N. and Broadbent, E. (2013). The psychosocial effects of a companion robot: A randomized controlled trial. *Journal of the American Medical Directors Association*, *14*(9), 661–667.

Ross, L. (1977). The intuitive psychologist and his shortcomings: Distortions in the attribution process. In L. Berkowitz (ed.), *Advances in Experimental Social Psychology* (pp. 173–220). New York: Academic Press.

Rozin, P., Lowery, L., Imada, S. and Haidt, J. (1999). The CAD triad hypothesis: A mapping between three moral emotions (contempt, anger, disgust) and three moral codes (community, autonomy, divinity). *Journal of Personality and Social Psychology*, *76*(4), 574–586.

Schott, G. (2011). Doodling and the default network of the brain. *The Lancet*, *378*(9797), 1133–1134.

Schwartz, B. (2000). Self-determination: The tyranny of freedom. *American Psychologist*, *55*(1), 79–88.

Seligman, M. E. P., Ernst, R. M., Gillham, J., Reivich, K. and Linkins, M. (2009). Positive education: Positive psychology and classroom interventions. *Oxford Review of Education*, *35*(3), 293–311.

Shweder, R. A., Much, N. C., Mahapatra, M. and Park, L. (1997). The 'Big Three' of morality (autonomy, community, divinity) and the 'Big Three' explanations of suffering. In A. Brandt and P. Rozin (eds), *Morality and Health* (pp. 119–169). London: Routledge.

Southwick, S. M., Gilmartin, R., Mcdonough, P. and Morrissey, P. (2006). Logotherapy as an adjunctive treatment for chronic combat-related PTSD: A meaning-based intervention. *American Journal of Psychotherapy*, 60(2), 161–174.

Stadler, G., Oettingen, G. and Gollwitzer, P. M. (2010). Intervention effects of information and self-regulation on eating fruits and vegetables over two years. *Health Psychology*, 29(3), 274–283.

Takeuchi, H., Taki, Y., Hashizume, H., Sassa, Y., Nagase, T., Nouchi, R. and Kawashima, R. (2012). The association between resting functional connectivity and creativity. *Cerebral Cortex*, 22(12), 2921–2929.

Tedeschi, R. G. and Calhoun, L. G. (1996). The posttraumatic growth inventory: Measuring the positive legacy of trauma. *Journal of Traumatic Stress*, 9(3), 455–471.

Tetlock, P. E., Kristel, O. V., Elson, S. B., Green, M. C. and Lerner, J. S. (2000). The psychology of the unthinkable: Taboo trade-offs, forbidden base rates, and heretical counterfactuals. *Journal of Personality and Social Psychology*, 78(5), 853–870.

Thierry, B., Steru, L., Chermat, R. and Simon, P. (1984). Searching–waiting strategy: A candidate for an evolutionary model of depression? *Behavioral and Neural Biology*, 41(2), 180–189.

Thomason, K. K. (2015). The moral value of envy. *Southern Journal of Philosophy*, 53(1), 36–53.

Torres, E. (2015). Philippines murder highlights the threat facing trade unionists. *Equal Times*, 24 March.

Tucker, A. W. (1983). The mathematics of Tucker: A sampler. *The Two-Year College Mathematics Journal, 14*(3), 228-232.

van de Ven, N., Zeelenberg, M. and Pieters, R. (2009). Leveling up and down: The experiences of benign and malicious envy. *Emotion, 9*(3), 419–429.

Wakefield, J. C. (1992). Disorder as harmful dysfunction: A conceptual critique of *DSM-III-R*'s definition of mental disorder. *Psychological Review, 99*(2), 232–247.

Watt, J. D. (1991). Effect of boredom proneness on time perception. *Psychological Reports, 69*(1), 323–327.

Waytz, A., Dungan, J. and Young, L. (2013). The whistleblower's dilemma and the fairness–loyalty tradeoff. *Journal of Experimental Social Psychology, 49*(6), 1027–1033.

World Health Organisation (2006). *World Health Statistics 2006.* Geneva: World Health Organisation.

Zhong, C.-B. and Liljenquist, K. (2006). Washing away your sins: Threatened morality and physical cleansing. *Science, 313*(5792), 1451–1452.

Index